PARENTEEN

Prakriti Prasad is a freelance journalist and columnist, who has worked with several leading publications, including *The Times of India*, *The Business Standard*, *The Indian Express* and *The Himalayan Times* for over two decades. As a relationship and meditation mentor and a parenting expert, she conducts wellness workshops and individual sessions with youngsters and adults. Well-versed in Hindustani classical music and kathak, she also plays the sitar. Prakriti is a diehard optimist who considers her ever-increasing circle of friends across the globe to be her greatest achievement in life. She lives in Kolkata.

PARENTEEN

How to nurture your adolescents in modern times

PRAKRITI PRASAD

Published by
Rupa Publications India Pvt. Ltd 2018
7/16, Ansari Road, Daryaganj
New Delhi 110002

Sales centres:
Allahabad Bengaluru Chennai
Hyderabad Jaipur Kathmandu
Kolkata Mumbai

Text and Illustrations Copyright © Prakriti Prasad 2018

Grateful acknowledgement is made to The Times of India Group for use of
copyrighted material from the author's column 'Parenteen'.

Illustrations courtesy: Manish Sharma, Patna (Bihar)

The views and opinions expressed in this book are the author's own and the facts are as
reported by her which have been verified to the extent possible, and the publishers are
not in any way liable for the same.

All rights reserved.

No part of this publication may be reproduced, transmitted, or stored in a retrieval
system, in any form or by any means, electronic, mechanical, photocopying, recording
or otherwise, without the prior permission of the publisher.

ISBN: 978-81-291-5119-3

First impression 2018

10 9 8 7 6 5 4 3 2 1

The moral right of the author has been asserted.

Printed in India by Thomson Press India Ltd., Faridabad

This book is sold subject to the condition that it shall not, by way of trade or otherwise,
be lent, resold, hired out, or otherwise circulated, without the publisher's prior consent,
in any form of binding or cover other than that in which it is published.

Contents

Prologue   vii

Introduction   ix

1. Communication is Crucial   1
2. Tone Down the Pressures   9
3. Curtail the Gadget-addiction   17
4. Accept Peers are Vital   25
5. Balance Privacy and Control   33
6. Comparisons are Self-defeating   42
7. Step Back a Little to Let Them Be   50
8. Stay Informed and Set Boundaries   58
9. Equip Them to Recognize and Fight Predators   66
10. Instil the Humility to Apologize and Seek Forgiveness   75
11. Spare the Rod and Know Your Child   83
12. Hold Your Horses When Mistakes Happen   91
13. Do Not Fear Their Fury   99
14. Calling Out the Demon Called Exam Stress   107
15. Enters the Dragon—Social Media   115
16. Emphasize on Safety Before Fun   124
17. It's Time to Tackle Underage Drinking   133

18. Train Them to Handle Adversity	142
19. Clip Complacency, Egg Them On to Dream	150
20. Instil Spiritual Grounding	159
21. Strive to Provide a Loving Home	168
22. Adapt Your Parenting Style	176
Epilogue	183
Acknowledgements	184
Suggested Readings	186

Prologue

She had sounded her cheerful self that morning. 'When do I get to see your book?' she had asked when I told her I was finally done with all the writing and editing work. I assured her I would be free and completely at her disposal when she and Dad came over next month. As we chatted for over 40 minutes making a list of things we were to do during their much awaited trip—the delicacies I would treat her to, that achaar I'd never realized I would suddenly be interested in making or the songs I needed to relearn from her—I never fathomed it would be my last conversation with my mother.

An hour later, she suffered a brain stroke and was gone after a brief struggle in the hospital.

I had been noticing the failing health of my elderly parents for quite some time, being painfully aware of the impending truth that lay therein. But when she actually passed away, it felt as if the umbilical cord had never been severed.

Now, as I absentmindedly reach out for the phone to call her as part of my morning regimen or crave to hear that excited, refreshing voice always the first one to wish me 'Happy New Year' or a 'Happy Birthday', I decide not to mourn the loss but celebrate the life of my mother.

In fact, the foundations of my parenting values were laid by my mother; a multi-faceted personality—she was a trained classical and folk singer and dancer who dabbled in acting too.

Besides the sitar, she played the tabla (a rarity for girls of her time), harmonium, dholak and the flute. Love for music was not just the centre force of her life but even the family she so lovingly nurtured. She ingrained the incredible power of music and love not just in her children but also in thousands of others who she taught as a guru. Another important quality I personified her with was the compassion she helped others with, often to the point of losing her sleep and peace of mind. *'Apne liye jiye toh kya jiye'* (What is the point in living just for yourself?) was her constant refrain even as she reminded us never to count our good deeds, *'Neki kar dariya mein dal!'* (Do good and forget it.) Her one-liners on life (like 'Time and Tide Wait for None' or 'Anger is Our Greatest Enemy') have come to form the basis of the character of all her four children.

She may no longer be with me in this world, but her learning and pearls of wisdom, I know, will constantly exhort me to not just be a better parent but a better human being too.

Most importantly, she will also remain the core of influence that helped me understand what it means to be a parent.

My mother, and hence this book.

Introduction

It was 2.30 a.m. as Smallie and I sat on the sofa in our living room wrapped in a warm tight hug, our cheeks still wet. As she looked at me affectionately and smiled, the first time in more than 48 hours, I felt a surge of relief inside. The situation had been defused. It had seemed to be a tough one this time—from getting her out of that 'leave-me-alone' attitude and staccato conversations to have her pour out her troubles and finally weighing out possible solutions. I checked the watch, only a couple of hours left for the alarm to go off for my morning regimen. But, it was worth every minute of the four hours we'd spent thrashing out the trouble that had threatened to rock the peace of my 15-year-old otherwise spirited girl.

'Mom, I wish all my friends had a mother like you. Actually, I really wish you could address every adolescent girl's distress like this,' she said through her glistening eyes. The mind quickly noted the compliment, rating it the best I'd received not just as a parent, but as an individual. It was a heady moment of victory I reckoned none of my exploits in the newspaper or on stage had ever evoked. I was overwhelmed not only by the flattering comment, but by the realization that I was on the right track, for my girl, despite all her distress, was able to empathize with other adolescents.

That was the genesis of my conviction to put down my thoughts and concerns about bridging distances between teenagers and parents in a book. Sometime later, overcome by my concern at the spurt in instances of teenage crime, suicides and other unscrupulous acts, I began writing a column on teenage parenting for *The Times of India* (Patna), where I'd begun my career as a trainee journalist. It was aimed at goading parents to get effectively involved with teens, and identify and relate to their insecurities and interests.

Spurred by the overwhelming response to my column as well as the urge to reach out to a wider cross section of parents as promised to my teen, I finally began work on this book. I must mention substantial sections of the ideas and content for this book draws from my newspaper columns and the research that I did for them. Of course for the book, I've delved deeper into the topics and sharpened my study to come up with case studies and possible solutions to a variety of teenage issues.

It goes without saying that **children are the biggest stress busters who bring cheer and meaning into our lives**. Nothing compares to the ecstasy of being blessed with a bundle of joy. As one begins the roller-coaster journey of parenthood, armed with enthusiasm and commitment to raise essentially good human beings, one experiences alternate moments of pride, happiness, tears and concern.

However, something seems to go terribly wrong soon after children begin celebrating their double-digit birthdays. It's when the hormones start kicking in that the lovable creatures become veritable monsters with the ability to turn you into all shades of red or purple with embarrassment and anger.

Suddenly, all the laughter and coochie cooing appear to get replaced by unwarranted outbursts, tears and verbal duels which constantly test your limits. As you stand outside the door that has been banged on your face, you sigh and wonder, 'Where did that cheerful happy-go-lucky child disappear?'

Teenage years can be stressful both for children who experience different physical and emotional changes, as well as parents who find themselves emotionally drained dealing with constant authority challenges, indifference and slammed doors. Comparing notes with friends and seeking the help of books and information on the Internet are only natural and logical solutions at hand.

In my endeavour to effectively handle our adolescent daughter, I pored over every available information and article I could lay my hands on, besides attending workshops, speaking to counsellors, psychologists and educators.

Over the years, I came to realize that while the behaviour of adolescents across the world remains more or less similar, Indian children born and brought up in a different sociocultural milieu from the West, have their own additional concerns. These seldom-addressed issues are what I have particularly laboured to attend to in this handbook.

ParenTEEN: How to Nurture Your Adolescents in Modern Times focuses on decoding the insecurities, dilemmas and interests of youngsters in order to understand them better. It emphasizes on keeping all channels of communication—the key to effective parenting—open. The book addresses a range of teenage issues pertaining to peer pressure, gadget addiction, underage drinking, teenage fury, exam stress and obsession with social media, to name a few.

The prime focus of this endeavour is on how to raise not

just happy, confident and humane children, but friends for life. It has practical pieces of advice, examples and real-life anecdotes pertaining to specific issues in each chapter which can help both parents and wards navigate the rough waters of teenhood.

I primarily write from my own experiences, information I gather during my interactions with teens (as they alone are the true experts on exploring the teenage thought process), apart from ones I have had with parents, teachers, psychiatrists, counsellors and spiritual leaders. Some of the names (marked with an *) have been changed to protect the identities on request.

An effective communication network is the most useful key to a healthy relationship. So, the foremost requirement for every parent is to spend quality time with youngsters. Encourage them to talk and share their thoughts, concerns or victories, no matter how small. That is the only way to get inside their minds and know where they are headed. So there are no shocks and uncanny surprises waiting for you on the way (see 'Stay Informed and Set Boundaries').

Another important step to positive parenting is to keep track of the vibrations we send our children. Are we being critical and condescending, are we being overindulgent, overtly suspicious or simply indifferent? Adolescents, I've realized, have this amazing attribute to catch the frequency of our vibrations and transform it into behaviour and actions—progressive or regressive. When our vibrations are of love and acceptance even while we correct them, there is a greater possibility of them actually listening (see 'Comparisons are Self-defeating').

So, I suggest we keep checking: 'Am I bringing out the best or the worst in my child?' Do not sweat if sometimes we

Introduction

unwittingly end up bringing out the worst in kids. Stop, change gears and remember not to harp on their past mistakes (see 'Spare the Rod and Know Your Child' and 'Hold Your Horses When Mistakes Happen').

Nevertheless, parents are after all human beings who are bound to goof up at times. But, we should have the courage to acknowledge our errors in judgement and promptly apologize to whoever we have erred, including our kids, without looking for excuses. When we hasten to own up to our mistakes and make suitable amends, we not just display strength of character, but also encourage children to emulate our behaviour (see 'Instil the Humility to Apologize and Seek Forgiveness').

As parents, we strive to provide the best food and education to our children. But, what we often miss out on is nourishing their soul power. Something we need to compulsorily put on our responsibility list is a commitment to nurture emotionally strong children who can handle setbacks and crises in life. For, only if the seed is strong will it be able to look after itself when it grows into a tree (see 'Train Them to Handle Adversity' and 'Instil Spiritual Grounding').

Meanwhile, we need to bear in mind that the relationship between parents has a profound impact on the mental and physical health of children. When husbands and wives function as a team, there are fewer instances of wayward behaviour or delinquency among youngsters. Sharing of parenting responsibilities between spouses, positive role-modelling and a loving environment together lead to healthy and self-reliant children ('Strive to Provide a Loving Home').

Parenting is, of course, something which comes naturally to

most adults the moment they are blessed with a newborn. But, positive parenting is an outcome of only concerted efforts at improving and evolving as parents ('Adapt Your Parenting Style').

Armed with a better understanding of teenage lives, instead of carrying on with archaic perceptions on parenting, we can hope to not just steer our children towards excellence, but also make friends of our teens for life.

1
Communication is Crucial

*'These are the good old days
you're going to miss in the years ahead.'*

—ANONYMOUS

Wasn't it just the other day that you sat your bundle of joy in front of the TV to watch *Playhouse Disney*? Within no time the kiddo moved to watching *Doremon* or *Phineas and Ferb*. And before you realized, they graduated to *Game of Thrones*. This journey may have been rather swift but certainly far from smooth. Moreover, the ride—every parent across the planet will agree—becomes particularly bumpy when their children hit adolescence.

No amount of educational qualifications or inherent smartness prepares you to handle the tumultuous teen years of your little ones who, till the other day, were your biggest stress busters. Since there is no set pattern to their behaviour, reactions and outbursts, one often wonders what bring the tears or squeals of excitement.

If it's any solace, every parent of a teen, with some exceptions of course, regularly seems to hit a wall when it comes to handling the kid during these volatile years. The anxiety levels understandably soar as the kid bangs the door shut after every tiff.

However, one of the biggest gaffes is when parents idolize their own adolescent years and berate the present generation. The truth is parenting teenagers has always been an arduous task from time immemorial. Greek philosopher Socrates, who lived in 500 BC, grumbled: 'Youth today have contempt for authority... they have bad manners... They contradict their parents and have no respect for older people.'

When we prefix our sentences with 'when we were children, we never...' while interacting with kids, we are sure to hit a communication block and ruin our relationship with them. It is this condescending attitude of most parents that creates barriers between them and their children. No wonder kids quickly tune them out of their range. While parents mope, children never listen.

Tune into Their Frequency

If we want to reach out to our kids, first and foremost, we need to step down from the pedestal of being an epitome of virtue. A free flow of communication is the most critical parenting tool. And for effective communication, it is imperative to identify ourselves with our kids, relate to their fears and concerns and show consideration.

A willingness to engage and listen is very crucial. Says Delhi-based public speaker and trainer Samir Deokuliar, 'As the kids grow, an important aspect of training and shaping their conviction is to have conversations and discussions. They could have opinions that need to be heard, discussed and then shaped.' One of the things that helped him greatly, he admits, was his frequent open discussions with his son who'd read a lot on atheism and multiple philosophies. 'I could not afford to be a closed door, but someone who listens and then contributes to the shaping,' adds the philanthropist who also offers spiritual service at the church.

Consciously making an effort not to scoff at their tastes or quirks, no matter how hideous they may seem, can go a long way in easing tensions between parents and teens. Focus on your children's interests and hobbies, probe what appeals to them and why, even if you do not understand them. When you begin taking an interest in their likes and dislikes, you actually open a new path of communication, a doorway to their mind domain. Besides, you never know, you may learn something new as they lead you to a whole new world of an unexplored genre of fun, music, books and films.

I remember sitting down one evening to watch the first part of *The Hunger Games* rather reluctantly after much pestering by my girl. However, I had such fun watching the movie with her as she explained the background and other implied references (for, she had read the book, too). Before I knew, I was hooked on to the series. But, more importantly, I understood our teen's sudden passion with knives which, of late, had been giving us sleepless nights.

It Pays to Hold Your Horses

One good thing about our teens now is they are far more vocal and expressive (maybe a tad more explosive too!) than their parents about what is appealing or repelling to their young minds. But, trouble brews when we, as adults, want them to conform to a line of behaviour that is more appropriate according to our standards. Consequently, tempers flare, decibels rise and unpleasantness prevails.

A handy tip, which I heard a few years ago, keeps replaying in my mind. 'Don't let your child's behaviour change yours,' said Jane Krill Thomson, an early intervention specialist at a parenting workshop. We often find ourselves losing our temper when confronted by aggression or adverse behaviour of children. According to Thomson, when your teen strays from the mutual code of conduct, instead of scowling, plant a positive look on your face. Stop yourself from shouting or yelling, for chances are either he/she will yell back or simply switch off. Explain that you do not like what is happening and leave the scene for at least a few minutes to cool off. Do not get dragged into a fight as it only defeats your purpose of parenting.

Keeping your voice low, but firm, even when the hyperventilating teen is straining every bit of your nerve, works wonders to tame the situation. Although remaining calm can be difficult amid extreme provocation, it is one skill every parent needs to gradually develop. Moreover, the way we handle each temper flare-up teaches them an important coping skill. They learn that solutions do not come through anger and excitement, but with a cool head. Remember, our goal is to equip children with strategies they will successfully use the rest of their lives.

Nevertheless, do not sweat if you do fly off the handle at times, for you are human. The important thing is to remember the useful hint and make peace at the earliest.

Get Them Talking

Now, let's get it straight—it's less important to say, but more important to listen. Once we get them talking, we know what is going on in their adolescent minds.

When Ananya returns from school in Pune, she offloads her mind and the day's events to her mother who claims to drop everything she may be doing to hear her out. Besides conveying a sense of priority to her teen, she gets an insight into her child's world. Children express their hopes, dreams, problems and fears through their conversations and reveal their psychological world. What most of us need to remember is there will be plenty of time to work, cook, clean or socialize, but only a handful of years of a daily conversation with our children.

However, there may be times when parents need to maintain a facade of nonchalance in order to goad hesitant teens into revealing their minds. Any invasive or loaded questioning can, sometimes, lead to clamming up of children. For instance, when my girl begins with 'Mom, I have to tell you something...', say, when I'm driving her to a friend's place, I try to keep my eyes glued to the windscreen and gently say 'shoot dear', even though the paranoid mother in me wants to slam the brakes and ask, 'What's gone wrong, now?'

Clinical psychologist and counsellor Dr Latika Prakash says encouraging youngsters to voice their views, fears and frustrations not just about studies, books, films, but also about tricky issues pertaining to friends, crushes or blunders, is good for mental health. It is always sensible to address their qualms, no matter how unfounded they may seem.

Listen Without Judgement

Parents need to remember that teenage years are difficult as children grapple with a whole lot of insecurities, fears and physical issues. So, when youngsters come to us, we need to listen openly. Reacting impulsively or setting off the parent alarm will only tend to dry up the communication channels.

Homemaker Antara* confesses she was tempted to reprimand her boy for giving undue attention to this girl in his coaching class, but practised restraint. 'For, I knew he would stop coming to me and go on to seek advice from inexperienced quarters.' Getting into the 'lecture mode' comes inadvertently to parents and that's when youngsters invariably switch off.

Teenagers do not always want us to give them advice. Sometimes, they just want to vent their feelings. Allow them to express themselves freely without the fear of repercussions like ridicule. Thoughtful questions or gentle prodding will let them process what they may be going through, helping them come up with their own solutions. Let them know that you think their feelings and ideas are worth sharing. They will learn to respect themselves and others because you have given them this important gift. Of course, this also fosters confidence in teens who are willing to pay an arm and a leg to be treated like adults.

Have Frequent Family Discussions

Experts claim that children form ideas and beliefs about themselves based on how their parents communicate with them. It is a good idea to have a fixed time for family meetings to discuss issues that are important to each member. Frequent chats, say, after meals, help children open up, as parents evince genuine interest in their day's activities. Inspirational speakers and authors Azim Jamal and Harvey McKinnon suggest starting this exercise early on when the children are young so that they remain 'open' in their teenage years. When parents regularly communicate with their children, particularly in the relaxed and tension-free atmosphere of the home, they get a peep into the latter's psychological world. As kids freely share their dreams and fears, opinions and misgivings, we get to know the dynamics of their thoughts.

Be sure, this way we are creating an amazing bonding for a lifetime with our children which they will love, cherish and pass on to their progeny.

2
Tone Down the Pressures

'Be kind, for everyone you meet is fighting a hard battle.'

—PLATO

It's true that the youngsters have never had it so good. People, who have witnessed the last few generations, point out that there has never been such freedom of expression, facilities for education and provisions for material luxuries as in the present times. Ironically, the stress levels of adolescents too have never been so high.

Youngsters today live under abominable pressures—pressure to look good, pressure to perform well in school, pressure to own the latest gadgets, pressure to fit in and be accepted—the list seems endless. The anxiety to perform well has never been more before. All these pressures are obviously taking a toll on their peace. No wonder incidence of unhappy children and young adults taking the extreme step is rising phenomenally.

'While as parents, we are providing for all their physical and material needs, we are missing out on preparing them to handle failures which are equally important in our lives,' points out Dr Roop Ghosal, a practising psychiatrist and counsellor who claims to have dealt with several cases where teenagers have been able unable to cope with pressure. With a poor 'coping mechanism' to handle failure as a part of life, learn from them and eventually rise above them, the children are bound to fall off the threshold, she adds.

Eighteen-year-old Anvesha[*], a fairly good student from Lucknow, who sat for her Class XII Board exams in 2017, was

Tone Down the Pressures

beyond her jittery self before the results. 'I will not live to see the next morning if I get anything less than 90 per cent,' she told her aunt, a friend of mine. The harried aunt was besides herself with concern for her niece as results are often unpredictable. She admonished the teen for the unscrupulous comment and tried to reason out in vain. For, no amount of pep talk seemed to ease her pre-result anxiety.

The friend's niece, incidentally, was not alone in her fixation on results. No sooner does the euphoria of having finished a major exam die down, anxieties about the results grip the examinees, sometimes even their parents.

In March 2017, a famous school in Kolkata dispatched an interesting letter to the parents of children to appear for their Board exams. It was a unique letter because at a time when almost every school focuses on tightening the pressure lever on students so as to get the best results, this one focused on arresting the stress levels of its students. The exclusive missive asked parents to bear in mind that amongst the examinees was an artist who didn't need to understand Math, a musician whose Chemistry marks won't matter or a sportsman for whom physical fitness would be more important than Physics. If your children do not score well, do not take away their self-confidence, said the letter. After all it's just an exam and they may be cut out for much bigger things in life. The note requested parents to assure their wards they would love them no matter what they scored. 'Please do this and watch your children conquer the world', ended the hearty communiqué.

I wish every parent, teacher and school principal adopts a similar attitude towards exams; and believe in the different inherent potentials of every kid—each one is born with the calibre to blossom, given the right direction and support.

Desist Being Pushy Parents

More often than not, I think it's the parents who fail to draw a line between exhorting their teens to perform well and pressurizing them with constant comparisons or warnings of unpleasant consequences.

Making our child's performance a prestige issue is yet another folly that we, even as matured adults, often commit unconsciously. A friend, I noticed, stopped socializing altogether when her son did not perform well in his Class X Boards. True, this is an age of so-called 'cut-throat competition' where every child needs to constantly prove his/her mettle against the other, but too much emphasis on marks can actually be detrimental to both the performance and the persona of the child in the long run.

Moreover, it has been proven time and again that underdogs and slow starters have eventually made it big in their lives. Be it scientists—Einstein, Edison and Newton were all below average in studies; remarkable world leaders such as Abraham Lincoln lost eight elections before becoming the president of the United States and Winston Churchill became the prime minister of England at 62 years of age after a lifetime of defeats; or artists of the calibre of Beethoven, Walt Disney and Charlie Chaplin who were all no shows initially.

Back home, the success stories of Bollywood stars Amitabh Bachchan, Rajinikanth or Akshay Kumar show how they struck gold only after initial setbacks and due to their persistent struggle.

So, while it is the onus of parents to provide all moral and logistic support to children in their respective endeavours, it is equally important to remember not to push them beyond their limits. For, blowing too much air into a balloon in order to make it bigger, sometimes only ends up bursting it.

Put Exams/Results in Perspective

Once the older generation, comprising parents and teachers, manage to change their mindsets about examinations—as being the ultimate verdict on our children's calibre—there's bound to be fewer nervous breakdowns, fewer suicides and fewer lives wrecked due to this annual phenomenon. This is because, more often than not, it's our own perception of studies, exams and careers that we consciously or unconsciously tend to pass on to our children, rather burden them with it.

While it's important for our children to set their goals high, it's equally crucial to prepare them to accept modifications in situations and go for a Plan B with equal gusto. Being rigid about ambitions and expectations is known to have landed children and their families in miserable circumstances.[1]

Successful entrepreneur and motivational speaker Sandeep Maheshwari—who himself, as it happens, struggled to build his life from a string of bad experiences as a mediocre middle-class youngster to become a youth icon today—gives a fascinating analogy regarding failures. He says it's like playing cricket on a pitch called 'life'. Every ball that we face is an opportunity

---

[1]'Exams Not the Final Verdict of Life', 19 March 2016. Source: The Times of India Group. © BCCL. All Rights Reserved

that keeps coming our way. Even if we miss one, we need to know the other one is coming right behind it. 'We may miss hitting, say, five consecutive balls. But for all you know, hit a "sixer" at the next one and make up for all the missed balls,' he says. Similarly, not succeeding in one event does not mean the end of life. One only needs to focus, understand the game and prepare for the next opportunity in order to strike a 'six', says the life coach.

Handle Unsatisfactory Results Deftly

Meanwhile, when the results of Boards or entrance exams are declared, it is bound to bring either cheer or distress to the families concerned. In case of an unsuccessful outcome, it's crucial for parents to become pillars of strength for their children. Remember, a dad's heart-to-heart chat or a mom's understanding hug reiterating their unflinching faith in the kid's calibre can work far more wonders than any amount of admonitions or entreaties to work harder.

It is imperative to remember that while on the one hand we must prepare our kids to take on all kinds of competitions and inspire them to scale records, on the other, we must not tie them down with the burden of our expectations. Let us train our children to focus more on their efforts and view failures as temporary setbacks to eventual success.

Shed Archaic Perceptions

- A 17-year-old computer engineering student jumped off the tenth floor of an apartment in Pune leaving a suicide note which said he wanted to pursue sociology,

not computer science. (12 June 2015)[2]
- Kolkata was rocked by the disappearance of a teenage medical student hailing from a small town in Bihar. He was traced to Jammu after nine days of gruelling search by police and a hapless family. The rank holder in the medical entrance exam claimed he was repulsed by the sight of blood and wanted to be an engineer, not a doctor as his father desired. (8 June 2015)[3]
- There has been a spate of deaths at the Indian Institutes of Technology (IITs) across the country. One student, who was saved from committing suicide in the capital, apparently never wanted to be an engineer. (Delhi, 29 March 2017)[4]

All these instances only underscore the fixation of parents about certain professions. Despite all our claims of being progressive and liberated parents of the twenty-first century, most of us are far from giving up our antiquated perceptions about careers. Even for parents who are highly educated and well-placed, it might be difficult to give up a mindset that supports the orthodox notion that children must grow up to be doctors

---

[2] '17-year-old boy jumps to death from 10th floor in Pune', *The Times of India City*, 12 June 2015, https://timesofindia.indiatimes.com/city/pune/17-year-old-boy-jumps-to-death-from-10th-floor-in-Pune/articleshow/47636697.cms

[3] 'Missing RG Kar student found in Jammu's Katra', *The Telegraph*, 16 June 2015, https://www.telegraphindia.com/1150616/jsp/calcutta/story_26036.jsp

[4] 'IIT-Delhi student attempts suicide', *The Hindu*, 29 March 2017, http://www.thehindu.com/news/cities/Delhi/iit-delhi-student-attempts-suicide/article17726124.ece

or engineers. I once overheard a conversation between two teenagers (daughters of our family friends) where they expressed their dislike towards being forced to study science despite a) the fact that they were doing well in it, and b) their interest in Literature and Economics.

It's sad how most of us are yet to get over the skewed notion that serious students take up Science, not-too-committed ones take Commerce while the mediocre ones go for Humanities. I was appalled to hear even a teacher once comment: 'Children opt for Humanities basically to escape from hard work as Intermediate Science, they know, is very tough and they will have to slog.' Most Indian parents, who influence their children to take up Science earmarking their careers as doctors and engineers, are evidently unaware of the growing prospects of alternate fields.

Parents must know exerting undue pressure on their child to pursue a career he has no interest in could certainly be the worst parenting decision of their life.

3
Curtail the Gadget-addiction

'The difference between technology and slavery is that slaves are fully aware that they are not free.'

—NASSIM NICHOLAS TALEB

We were some twenty-five families of friends and colleagues on a river cruise on the Hooghly on a sunny winter morning. While the adults were soaking in the beautiful view on the deck, sailing across iconic bridges and temples along with a live band, we suddenly realized all the children were missing. To our dismay, we found them all cooped up in the air-conditioned hall below, busy on their smartphones, iPads and gaming consoles, oblivious to the live music and nature's beauty around.

Addiction to the idiot box, laptop or cell phone is one universal phenomenon that practically every household appears to be grappling with in different measures. One would never have imagined the seemingly harmless babysitter (read televisions/iPads) that new moms readily hand over their toddlers to, would one day transform into such a menace devouring their child's time for outdoor activities and study.

The increasing presence of technology in the lives of children is, in fact, causing them to display borderline autistic behaviour, point out experts across the world. Constant use of smartphones, television screens and computer monitors wherein children engage in virtual reality is the reason behind problems related to maintaining attention and understanding emotions or facial expressions, explain psychiatrists.[5]

Sunil Jha, a banker posted in Kolkata and sailing in the same boat as most parents of teenagers, calls this the 'TMC generation'—not for their leanings towards the Trinamool Congress (West Bengal's leading party) but for compulsorily thriving on television, 'mobile' phones and computers in variable degrees. We cannot agree more as the present generation has indeed come to swear by these three gadgets. They would rather give their precious time and attention to any of these than indulge in 'unnecessary' socializing with relatives and family friends.

Genesis of Addiction

Nevertheless, kids are not entirely to be blamed for this addiction to screens. Besides being born into this jet age of high-speed technology, it's often the overzealous parents who help foster this obsession for gadgets early on in life. Isn't it common to come across adults who readily hand over their smartphones to infants either to befriend them or, in case of parents, to keep them entertained? Some parents, in fact, gloat with pride at their toddlers' expertise in handling all kinds of gadgets at such an early age. What they overlook is not just the health hazard as they expose their young ones to harmful emissions from these gadgets, but also the genesis of addiction that they are laying so unwittingly.

---

[5]Richard E. Cytowic, 'There is a New Link between Screen-time and Autism', 29 June 2017, https://www.psychologytoday.com/blog/the-fallible-mind/201706/there-is-new-link-between-screen-time-and-autism

Meanwhile, as the children grow up, dependence on technology and screens becomes unavoidable. In most schools today, all circulars and assignments have to be accessed, researched and submitted on the Internet. In fact, there are some schools which have switched to using tablets instead of textbooks in order to reduce the weight of the students' school bags. While cell phones have become a necessity to ensure the whereabouts and safety of children, television is considered as essential as a refrigerator. After all, it disseminates a whole lot of information too. I was pleasantly amused to hear a family friend credit his son's feat at cracking the IIT, not to his coaching institute, but to his addiction to the Discovery Channel.

While it's difficult to negate the benefits of gadgets in our everyday lives, the crucial question is how much is too much.

Moderation is the Key

'Excess of anything is bad', happened to be my mother's constant refrain when we were kids. That is what I, as a mom, apply when it comes to technology in our lives. We follow some basic rules for the use of gadgets at home. For instance, television viewing is limited to weekends and holidays. Although long aware of the health hazards of excessive television watching, we took the tough decision when we realized the idiot box was beginning to decide the moods of our children—primarily causing aggression and irritability. I confess it took a lot of patience and persistence for our unpopular decision (often criticized by relatives and neighbours) to become an accepted norm in the family.

One needs to establish clear rules that will keep teens safe and help them make good choices with video games, cell phones,

TVs and computers. In fact, too much screen time has been linked to a variety of problems. It raises the risk of obesity, interferes with social activities and family time and may lead to Internet addiction which is increasingly being considered almost at par with the dependence on alcohol and cigarettes. As informed adults, we need to work out a personalized system of checks and balances on all the gadgets around.

Clearly Outline Screen Timings

The number of waking hours that our teens spend staring at screens—be it for texting or watching videos on iPads—is a sure cause of worry. But we can offset the negative impact of technology in their lives by having pre-negotiated screen timings so as to avoid repeated conflicts with our kids.

Ensure all screens are switched off while studying. For, most teens have a habit of multitasking (either texting or watching a video) while studying. Although getting them to give up their cell phones completely may be a difficult proposition as they seem to guard it with their lives, convince them to keep the phones away while studying.

It is equally imperative for parents and guardians to monitor the Wi-Fi or Internet surfing of children. Fifteen-year-old Sana* is unable to wake up early as she stays up till the wee hours of the morning watching movies and videos on YouTube, says her grandmother nonchalantly. Ironically, the elderly lady does not find it alarming as she believes that's the way it is for all youngsters today.

By no chance should one leave children unsupervised when they are surfing the Internet after the household has retired for the day. They might tend to indulge in unscrupulous browsing out of sheer curiosity. Also, make sure the TV gets turned off at a set time at night. Aberrations, though not too many, can be made for certain events, say, for watching a crucial match or so.

Ensure Screen-free Meals

Watching television while eating is clearly ticked off by doctors and psychologists alike for it is known to cause overeating or binge eating. Moreover, it fosters disconnect with the food as well as the people with whom we eat—family, friends or relatives.

During meals, make it a family rule to switch off all screens, be it television, WhatsApp on cell phones or the iPad. There should be no texting whether at home or at restaurants. Use the time instead to have light-hearted and fun-inducing conversations. Laughter and banter are known to work well for digestion. 'As teens, we used to have these marathon sessions of laughter at the dining table after the meals,' recounts Delhi-based teacher and a mother of three, Namrata. 'In those frugal times, no matter how basic the food would be, we always used to get up with the feeling of having had a hearty meal,' she adds fondly.

Encourage Physical Activity

A major outcome of addiction to gadgets is inadequate physical activity for the young generation. It is really sad to come across near empty playgrounds and parks in every locality in almost every city. Most youngsters today prefer to hang out in malls and pubs instead. Children, who do choose to go down to playgrounds, never forget to bring along their latest gadgets either to flaunt or discuss the features and the latest apps.

Encourage children to play with friends, both indoor and outdoor games, or enrol in, say, yoga, karate or dance classes. Participating in sports, music, theatre and painting, among other things, can keep them constructively involved and away from technology. Mumbai-based HR professional Shilpi Deokuliar claims her sports freak son has no time on his hands for any gadget. 'Early mornings before school are booked for marathon and football lessons, alternately. In the afternoon, he quickly finishes off homework and revision work before leaving for his cricket training. He returns home a spent force and hits the bed after a quick meal,' she chuckles.

Plan Gadget-free Family Activities

Every once in a while it is a good idea to have a screen-free day for the family. On these days, do not allow anyone to use electronic items. Involve everyone in activities that do not require electronic gadgets, like playing a board game, antakshari, dumb charades or going for a family picnic or hike.

Wellness expert and stress management consultant Nandini Choudhury Brahmachari recommends having 'no cell phone parties' for the teens wherein youngsters are required to compulsorily leave behind their smartphones and focus purely on food, physical games and dance instead of texting or clicking selfies.

Role Modelling is Crucial

And last but not least, it is important to remember that children are often our mirror images. We first need to clean up our own acts in order to bring about positive changes in their lives. As parents, we have to role model the behaviour we want to see in our youngsters. We cannot ask kids to cut back on their screen time if we sit glued in front of the telly watching endless daily soaps and news programmes, texting while driving or scurrying to check our phones at every beep.

Unfortunately, we all know bad habits are easier to imitate. It helps to know that our children are watching us intently and wittingly or unwittingly tend to follow in our footsteps. That is to say, the onus of setting a decent example of using technology to our advantage, instead of letting it rule our lives, rests on us too.

4
Accept Peers are Vital

'A friend is a gift you give yourself.'

—ROBERT LOUIS STEVENSON

As children enter adolescence, parents unwittingly cease to be their role models. The opinions and reactions of parents suddenly begin to hold less sway on their minds even as they seek support and inspiration from other quarters—mainly friends.

This end of the honeymoon period with kids comes as a shocker to parents. While some helplessly watch their bundles of joy drift away from them, others try to tighten their hold on them. Unfortunately, the tighter the hold, the more intense is the effort to break free from the 'tutelage of parents'. Consequently, what follows in most households with teenagers is frequent unrest, run-ins and tears. In some, there is often a full-fledged war going on between the parents and youngsters.

First and foremost, parents need to accept the fact that their children's world will widen as they grow. And it's more than healthy if they begin to see their world beyond family, relatives or immediate neighbours. As they begin interacting with people, they are bound to be drawn more towards children their own age (also called peers in common jargon) for the simple reason that they can relate to each other better.

As parents, we all have friends and love spending time with them. However, we fail to understand why peer group suddenly becomes so important to our children that they go to the extent of rebelling against their own families. According to psychologists, the meaning of friendship changes as children get into their teens. While earlier they needed friends for having someone to play with, they now want someone to confide in or share their feelings.

Advantages of Peers

Even though as parents, we would like to believe that we can provide all the emotional support that our teens need, that is not always possible. We cannot always reach how they perceive situations, we cannot always comprehend their fears and insecurities or even the reasons for their joyous mood. Peer influence during adolescence, point out experts, is quite normal and tends to peak around age 15, after which it begins to decline. As parents of teens, it will be helpful to bear in mind that peers give our youngsters a sense of belonging and an increased sense of self-confidence.

'Friendship for teens, particularly girls, is a need and is fundamental to how they see themselves,' points out Ranjana Roy, a senior counsellor at a Birla School in Kolkata. And facing the influence of friends represents an important developmental step for teens on their way to becoming adults with an independent mind, she adds.

Most teens support each other in a way that helps them be a sounding board for issues such as relationships, school, work and conflict with parents. In fact, a number of counsellors I interviewed reiterated that healthy friendship can positively influence the scholastic, social and personal aspects of a teenager's life.

Sixteen-year-old Sheena[*] was struggling to keep pace with her Physics teacher in class. She could not understand the theorems and was too shy to interrupt the teacher and ask her to explain. So, when her bench partner Gayatri* realized her predicament and offered to explain the concepts during lunch breaks, Sheena was overwhelmed beyond words. That was the beginning of their friendship too.

Besides acting as great confidence builders, teenagers tend to provide solace and support to each other to help cope with trouble, whether at home or in school. Nevertheless, friends can often be judgemental and the cause of heartache too, especially when conflict or alienation occurs.

Peer Pressure can be Stifling

While peers are known to exercise substantial influence on youngsters across cultures throughout the world, what becomes a matter of concern for parents is when children blindly follow their friends. They often refuse to heed their parents' or their own sense of reasoning and judgement, only to be accepted by people their age whether at school and college or in the locality or a club. Peer influence goads youngsters choose something they wouldn't otherwise do like indulging in drinking, smoking or bullying, merely because they want to feel accepted and valued by their friends.

Wanting to be more like their friends is a normal part of being a teenager, say experts. But some kids tend to give in more to peer pressure simply because they want to quickly fit in a group, or because they worry other kids might make fun of them if they don't follow suit. Still others go along because they are curious to try something new that many are doing. This 'everyone-is-doing-it' notion can greatly influence some children to leave their better judgement behind.

Peer influence might result in children
- Behaving in a certain way
- Changing the way they talk, use words or slangs
- Choosing the same dressing style or hairdo as their friends
- Listening to the same music or watching the same TV shows as their friends
- Trying out risky things or breaking rules
- Dating, smoking, using alcohol or other drugs
- Working harder at school, or not working as hard

Though peer pressure affects all children, some are more likely to be negatively influenced by peers—for instance, children who have poor self-esteem or those who feel they have few friends or those with special needs. 'Children who have strong self-esteem are better at resisting negative peer influence,' observes Nandini Choudhury Brahmachari. 'If kids are happy with who they are, they will less likely be influenced by other people. Self-esteem helps in establishing good relationships and positive friendships,' she adds. Coping well with peer pressure is about getting the right balance between being themselves and fitting in with their group.

Negative peer pressure, when not handled sensitively in time, can prove detrimental and sometimes even fatal for a youngster. Brahmachari narrates a bizarre incident of aggressive body shaming (mocking a person for his/her body shape or size) of a 17-year-old girl in a small town of West Bengal. Unable to handle the humiliation and mockery by friends and peers both in person and on the social media, the emotionally vulnerable teen committed suicide. Her poor semi-literate parents were absolutely clueless about their daughter's ordeal which made her flip the edge.

How to Tame Peer Influence

A bright and intelligent youngster, Shaurya* is the favourite of all teachers at his school in Muscat. But his mother, a noted academic herself, agonizes over the fact that 'he prefers to hang out with underachievers and underperformers all the time'. All admonitions to change his friends' circle have fallen on deaf ears as the defiant teen shoots back: 'Where is it written that underdogs and underachievers should stick around with only their kind? What if I can bring about an improvement in their grades?' The otherwise articulate mother is left groping for words.

Teenagers often end up testing their parents' patience and nerve. And when it is a matter concerning their friends and companions, they are particularly defensive. Parents need to know this is wet ground as criticism of pals is often taken personally. Understandably, the reaction of most parents is also identical—categorically warning their kids to stay clear of the friend(s) they think can have a bad influence on them. But far from grasping their concern, children tend to react more aggressively causing substantial heartburn.

Friends make a man, they say. The company one keeps has a major bearing on his character and personality. So, parents certainly need to keep a watchful eye on the companions of their children in order to curb the negative impact of peer pressure, but at the same time let them choose their friend circle.

Here are some guiding principles for parents to monitor peer influence:

Ensure a loving and caring home

When the relationship with teens is based on trust and understanding, they will be less likely to give in to negative peer pressure. Encourage your child to come to you without the fear of being rebuked.

Know their friends

It's always a good idea to get to know your teen's friends. Befriending them and their parents or inviting them over to your home frequently gives you a peek into their lives. I, for one, can vouch for the efficacy of this tool as I make it a point to create my own chemistry with all my daughter's friends and their mummies. So while I know the circle in which she socializes, she doesn't feel any need to hide facts or outings with them.

Discuss your concerns

It is crucial to lay down specific rules about friends and share your concerns, if any, in a calm tone with your children. You should try to elicit more information like asking the child why he/she likes a friend who concerns you. Instead of banning that friend outright, starting a dialogue can yield better results.

Parents should thoroughly assess their kids' friends, maintains Laurence Steinberg, author of *You and Your Adolescent*. It's better to start early and express opinions. Once a child reaches adolescence, friends may wield more influence than authority figures. So, simply saying you are not allowed to hang out with a particular friend any more may be met with resistance.

Educate how to handle negative peer pressure

Teach kids strategies to recognize and deal with negative peer pressure like when to say a polite yet firm no. Parents can also help children anticipate situations of peer pressure like declining alcohol at a party or trying out a risky act just to be reckoned as 'cool'. Strategies to help a child save face while still avoiding an activity or having a prepared response can greatly help a teen. Let's say you allow your teenage daughter to go to a party at a friend's house. Discuss the scenarios when it will be better for her to leave.

Harness their conscience

Groom your children's conscience so it can act as their police in the absence of parental guidance, say, in the company of a bunch of heady youngsters. Emphasize that they should never go ahead with something suggested by friends that makes them uneasy. They are probably about to do something wrong which could possibly have a lasting negative effect on their lives.

Underline the fact that good friends not just turn you into leaders, but also good human beings, and it is not like you have to fit in.

Finally, it is essential to understand that while the importance of peers during adolescence maybe at its peak, parents still remain the most vital source of influence in their lives.

5
Balance Privacy and Control

*'My mother had a great deal of trouble with me,
but I think she enjoyed it.'*

—MARK TWAIN

I was interviewing Meira Kumar for a coffee table book on her father, Babu Jagjivan Ram, the notable freedom fighter and parliamentarian. As I inquired about her memories of Babuji during her growing up years, the sexagenarian, who was then the speaker of the Lok Sabha, broke into a fond smile. 'Babuji respected my privacy so much that he would never enter my room even if it was open,' reminisced Kumar, 'he would stand behind the curtains and knock or cough if he needed to speak to me.'[6]

During our conversation, what struck me immediately was this realization that privacy was so crucial for a teen even half a century back. Today, of course, it is considered to be a principal need for every youngster for which, metaphorically speaking, they are willing to give their right arm. Their room is their haven and their 'space' sacrosanct. The poor parents often stand gaping trying to digest this transformation of their cheerful kid who, until the other day, would jump into their beds and demand to be cooed and cuddled.

A friend and television artist on a hiatus from work to be with her only son was in for a rude shock when she realized

---

[6]See Prakriti Prasad, 'Leading on With His Baton', in *Jagjivan Ram 1908–1986, Babuji: More than a Messiah of Dalits*, Jagran Prakashan Limited, 2014, p. 25.

the centre of her attention would rather be left alone. He had become so used to his space that he found her concerns meddlesome.

The issue of privacy is clearly a source of friction in most teen households. While parents understand the changing needs of adolescents who go through a phase of physical and mental metamorphosis, what bothers them is their children's leave-us-alone attitude. As the mother of a teen daughter, I too have reservations about bolted doors and communication barricades that youngsters sometimes create around them and hasten to resolve the issue as soon as possible.

The kids, on their part, plead they need privacy to do their own thing—like listen to their kind of music, write journals, watch videos, movies or chat with friends who they feel are better equipped to handle their issues than the grown-ups. 'Like every adult, we too need our personal space to do things we please and keep some things which only we are privy to instead of sharing with parents or anyone for that matter,' points out 17-year-old Rhea, a college student from Delhi.

Expert Speak

Experts agree that youngsters should be given due privacy depending on their age. 'When we give our teens the privacy they need, they become more independent and self-confident,' feels Dr Roop Ghosal who particularly works with youngsters. At the same time, parents need to share with their children the dangers of keeping them in the dark about their blunders and mistakes. Ghosal suggests striking a balance between being aware of what the teens are doing and trusting them to have some private matters. Of course, parents need to trust their instincts in order to decide when to step in.

According to Samir Deokuliar, most parents miss the mark by either being super controlling all their lives or being a bit too gracious when they should not be. 'One of the most common things I have noticed in India is when kids are small, they are allowed to really control the parents' lives (a classic example is running around feeding them rather than making them sit in one place, listen and be fed) and then when they are growing up the parents get upset when they begin to make their own choices (such as who they should marry, what job they should take or what they should believe) as the parents then want to control everything.' Deokuliar claims the order is wrong. The goal of good parenting is for us to control when kids are very small and release them when they are older so that they can stand on their own convictions.

'Adolescents should be given some amount of privacy based on their needs and behaviour, but under the watchful eye of parents,' points out Dr Latika Prakash, 'or else this privacy can become detrimental to the child's healthy growth.' An alarming trend noticeable in almost every family is that of adolescents staying up till late in the night 'doing their thing' on iPads, laptops or cell phones. In fact, most parents have come to accept these as normal demands of this generation. 'Kids in the age group of 10–18 years should not be allowed total freedom either on the Internet or in their outings with friends,' says Prakash, an associate professor who counsels adolescents.

What is clearly evident is that while teens need some amount of privacy, parents need to strike a subtle balance between giving them 'their space' and remaining sensibly clued on to their activities and shenanigans. It is indeed a tightrope walk for parents gauging when to let them be and when to barge in and exercise their veto.

Jammu-based software professional Naina Bhandari[*] confesses she was always paranoid about what was cooking in her teen daughter's mind. So, she would often hunt out the journal that she found her kid vigorously writing into every now and then. There was, of course, a major showdown when the daughter found out her mother had been reading her journal, but as a consequence, she stopped writing altogether. 'I regret my paranoia as it killed my girl's desire to write a journal,' rues the mother now.

How much privacy is healthy for children is, anyway, a matter of debate among parents and counsellors. But there are some helpful pointers for parents to keep in mind about when to let kids be on their own and when to call the shots.

Encourage openness

A worrisome trend among youngsters is almost all of them prefer to be holed up in their rooms with computers and iPads or watching their favourite television series, alone or with friends. The concept of sitting out with the family in the living room is almost passé, all in the name of 'privacy'. And then parents wonder why their kids did not bother to participate in family activities or how they got involved with something they had no idea they were doing.

In order to encourage children to spend more time with them, first and foremost, parents need to give up their condescending attitude and tendency to sermonize them all the time. Having a lighter, chilled out atmosphere in the house where there is fun and openness about every big and small issue, can go a long way in goading youngsters to come out of their shells. Once again, having frequent, frank conversations about anything and everything ensures children have fewer secrets to keep from their parents. Psychologists point out that youngsters, who have strong ties with their parents, are less likely to indulge in unscrupulous behaviour like using drugs or alcohol.

Have clear rules

Have a discussion with your children about how much privacy and leeway is acceptable to you as a family and elucidate with reasons. Explain that different children from diverse family backgrounds may have varied levels of liberty and privacy. What works for one family may not work for another. Shazia Ahmed*, a professor of English in Lucknow claims that while she is game for her teenage son to bring over friends and chill in his room if he pleases, she is averse to letting him go on sleepovers to other people's places. 'I have standing instructions to my staff to pamper them with whatever delicacies the boys want so they have fun inside the house and I can keep a tab on their activities,' says the conscientious mother.

Be unambiguous from the very beginning about the fact that their privacy on all devices like smartphones, laptops or iPads is limited—that you will check them regularly. It is helpful to explain that you are setting these rules not because you do not trust them, but because it is your responsibility to keep them safe.

Ensure privacy is a privilege

It is sensible for parents to make it clear to their children early on that privacy is a privilege which has to be earned by consistent and respectful behaviour. And just like a licence, it can be revoked for irresponsible behaviour like lying or breaking trust. If studies and school work begin to suffer as a result of, say, spending unlimited time texting or gaming, do not hesitate to take them away. But ensure you return the privileges when your kid makes suitable amends in his behaviour.

Practise selective Internet privacy

Youngsters across the world unwittingly share a wide range of information about themselves on social media. In fact, most sites encourage sharing of information and ensure expansion of networks. What's more, these sites keep changing their privacy rules so often that it can be difficult to keep up. On Facebook, for instance, unless you specifically opt out, your status updates, videos and images can be seen by anyone—not just your friends or friends of friends.

While we can't keep children from accessing the Internet either for their school work or leisure, it is important to impress upon them never to share their passwords with anyone—even their friends. Even if teens do not share their passwords with you, make them agree to let you browse through their Internet history, mail or chat account details. Most psychologists and counsellors agree it is imperative for parents to frequently monitor the Internet presence of their children.

Be wary of unsupervised parties

Although teenage parties with fun, food, music and dance have been in vogue for decades, they have assumed scandalous proportions off late. Besides birthdays, there are pre-exam and post-exam parties for the kids to unwind. Unsupervised by any adult, most of these teenage revelries which can be held at bizarre places have a free flow of alcohol. Kolkata was rocked by the death of a 16-year-old boy of a famous school at one such wacky birthday party in the parking lot of an upscale locality. The CCTV footage showed the teens carrying liquor bottles under their arms.[7]

It is important for parents to speak to the host before allowing children to go for such parties. One must always check whether an adult will be present and be categorical about any use of alcohol. Be assured you are not being a killjoy, only ensuring the safety of your child.

Read the Warning Signs

It is always sensible to be observant and alert about the body language of kids. Teens, no doubt, need privacy, but there are times when one is required to snoop around and invade their privacy. When youngsters display sudden loss of appetite, erratic change of behaviour in terms of anger, depression or a tendency to hurt themselves or others, it's time to take charge of the

---

[7]'Kolkata: Initial evidences indicate Abesh Dasgupta was hit accidentally, say police', *DNA*, 26 July 2016, http://www.dnaindia.com/india/report-kolkata-initial-evidences-indicate-abesh-dasgupta-was-hit-accidentally-sayspolice-2238200

situation. Attentive parenting requires you to immediately swing into action and get kids the help they need before something dreadful happens.

6

Comparisons are Self-defeating

> *'We are what we repeatedly do.*
> *Excellence then is not an act, but a habit.'*
>
> —ARISTOTLE

Several decades ago, a detergent advertisement with the tagline 'How come her sari looks whiter than mine' became an instant hit on both electronic and print media. The commercial's creative director had hit the bullseye by grasping the pulse of millions—to be better than others. This is exactly how we gauge our children's achievements as well as ours, where we/they stand in comparison with others. No matter how big a child's triumph is, it always tends to lose its sheen if the neighbour's son has a bigger feat to boast of.

'Mom I scored 95 per cent in Mathematics today,' says your youngster returning home from school. After congratulating him/her at his success, your next sentence invariably is, 'What was the highest?' There's nothing wrong in knowing the highest score, but trouble begins when you start interrogating your child, 'Where did you lose those five marks?'; 'How could you afford to do those silly mistakes?'; 'Didn't you promise to revise your paper twice?'. Within five minutes you have managed to underscore the child's accomplishment, all because another child scored a couple of marks more.

Another scenario could be when your child may not be a great achiever either in academics or in extracurricular activities. Once again, your constant reprimands—'Look at Tania aunty's son, he gets a scholar badge every year', or 'Learn something from your older brother, he manages to win medals in sports as well as in studies'—are unlikely to get him motivated to perform any better. If at all, they will only be detrimental to his/her performance.

Practically speaking, parents can either build or break the confidence and self-esteem of their children. Ironically, the intention behind comparisons by most parents is merely to goad children to achieve or perform better. But more often than not, the message that gets conveyed is loaded with negative energy which only tends to worsen the situation.

At the outset, parents, guardians and teachers need to clearly recognize three facts. Firstly, no two lives are similar. Since all children come with their set of skills, inherent strengths and weaknesses, expecting them to have an identical success rate is substantial cause for conflict. Secondly, adolescents develop innumerable insecurities as they grow up, those pertaining to looks, complexion, skin, expression or excellence in academics and extracurricular activities. Now, it is up to the parents and teachers whether to aggravate these insecurities or work at removing them in order to make the teens comfortable with themselves. And thirdly, using competition, punishment or anger as your motivational markers is unlikely to propel your child on the highway to success. They only result in causing manifold stress, anxiety and conflict both for the children as well as their parents.

Impact of Comparison

Dr Roop Ghosal maintains that Indian parents, by far, are the toughest to please. 'They want their children to be super boys and girls as they expect them to be the best looking, best dressed, best in studies, sports or other talents,' feels Ghosal. Adolescence is, anyway, a tough stage for children as they come to terms with physiological, hormonal and emotional changes. Constant comparisons with friends or siblings only tend to compound their ordeal, is her observation.

Comparing children has multiple negative impacts on their overall behaviour and performance:

- An instant outcome is resentment for the person praised.
- Sibling rivalry is often recognized by experts as a major fallout of relentless, and sometimes unwitting, comparisons with brothers and sisters by parents and even teachers.
- Persistent evaluation in terms of others causes lowering of self-esteem among youngsters.
- Children tend to feel unappreciated and unloved which in turn spurs a string of negative emotions harmful for both health and performance.
- Consistent comparisons can also prompt a 'couldn't-care-less' attitude among children.
- As the child perceives you are pitted against him, he feels distanced from you.

Focus on Strengths

It is imperative to remember that harping on the negative will only make it grow in leaps and bounds. For, energy flows wherever attention goes and so the trait we focus on grows.

Aniket*, 15, had anger issues. Although reasonably good at studies and a brilliant drummer, he would fly off his handle anywhere, any time with the slightest provocation. The otherwise loving parents unwittingly found themselves incessantly discussing his volatile temperament. They even tried to make light of the problem by jokingly calling him 'the angry young man of the family'. Instead of focusing on his strengths, like his diligence in studies and skill with the drums, the constant attention on his weakness ensured he was repeatedly reminded of being an angry boy.

Parents sometimes tend to inadvertently harp on their children's flaws and wrongs in front of others, hoping they would wane. But to our dismay, the opposite happens due to the simple reason that attention only helps them multiply. We need to remember to 'stop watering the plant we want to die', point out spiritual masters.

Interestingly, both pranic healing and Reiki work on this belief of focusing on positive energy whether in healing an ailment or a vice or ensuring success in one's endeavours.

Join Forces to Combat Weakness

If your youngster is weak in a particular area, say, academics, communication or life skills, instead of berating him, encourage him to cope with the weakness or register external support like hiring a tutor. Focus on harnessing his capacity and help him reach his optimum capability. Most importantly, set higher benchmarks for him so that he betters himself, not against any other child. For instance, during a race, athletes are trained to look straight instead of looking at other runners. Going by a similar logic, a racing horse has blinkers to keep its eyes focused on what is ahead, rather than what is at the side or behind when racing round a racecourse. Parents, particularly Indians, need to realize that academic performance is not the single important benchmark to perceive whether a kid would grow up to be successful in life. Your friend's daughter may have scored 95 per cent in the Board exams, but your daughter may be very good at speaking or connecting with people and subsequently make it big in life as a great communicator.

Practise Giving Up Critical Thoughts for a Day

Try to let go of preconceptions and negative ideas at least for a day, to begin with. Vow spending the day practising love, acceptance and kindness not just in response to kindness, but even when the teen is being unkind. I know being compassionate appears a difficult proposition when your teen is straining your patience. But practise doing it as an experiment and observe the difference. When we move away from judging our kids, apart from doing away with the disharmony in our minds and the household, we teach an important lesson to them—of not being judgemental towards others.

Believe in a Positive Premise

There was a time when our teen slipped in her academic performance in school. Some of her teachers who had known her to be a diligent child since junior school were categorical in their assessment during the Open House (also called Parent-Teacher Meeting or PTM). As we reached home with a brooding silence having prevailed in the car, our girl waited with bated breath to be hauled up by us individually. I started, 'You know honey, I don't disbelieve your teachers, but one thing I know for sure is you are going to do very well in life. And that's what matters to the both of us.' The look on our girl's face was a canvas of emotions revealing happiness, relief, remorse and a subtle determination.

I sincerely believe parents need to operate with a positive premise about their children. When we expect the best in our conscious minds, the subconscious goes on to faithfully reproduce our habitual thinking, says Dr Joseph Murphy in his commendable work, *The Power of Your Subconscious Mind*. Conversely, if one keeps fearing the worst, there is a high possibility of the worst to actually materialize. Anyway, as we function with a persistent optimism, a lot more gets accomplished for there is no disharmony created by perpetual bickering and criticism.

Help Them Visualize Success

Parents can help their teens visualize where and how they want to see themselves in future. This is what the experts term as the power of visualization which acts as a stirrup for realization of goals. 'One of the quickest ways to obtain anything you set your heart on is to practise visualization,' says Al Koran in his bestselling book, *Bring Out the Magic in Your Mind*.

Creative visualization is a mental practice that uses imagination to make dreams and goals come true. The technique has been successfully tapped by high achievers across the world, be it Tiger Woods, Muhammad Ali, Jim Carrey or Oprah Winfrey, to name a few. Experts universally agree, when used in the right way, effective visualization can improve our lives and attract success and prosperity.

Be as vivid as possible so kids begin to feel the thrill of accomplishment. This visual of success created in their mind's eye can act as a great stirrup to escalate their endeavours. Meanwhile, the law of nature and the power of attraction will combine to make these visions materialize into reality.

It is proven that youngsters who possess vision and the drive to achieve their dreams have higher resilience and are more likely to make wise choices in life. And as parents of prospective achievers, we have to ignite that fire in their bellies. Meanwhile, parents and teachers must compulsorily abandon archaic methods of motivation which tend to bring down the morale of their wards and adopt more innovative and encouraging tools instead. Only then can we hope to have fewer instances of depression, suicides or nervous breakdowns in our children's worlds.

Be Generous with Your Praises

Today, most people believe that their achievements are best savoured only when posted online for the world to see. Whether you indulge in online bragging or not, make sure you convey your genuine happiness at your kid's achievements to him/her personally. Psychiatrists and counsellors concede that showing appreciation not only for the children's achievements, but their efforts too, go a long way in building their confidence. Besides, praising their persistence or progress even if they need to do much more tends to keep them on the job. And children become model citizens only when they feel appreciated by people who matter.

7

Step Back a Little to Let Them Be

> *'The people who get on in this world are the people who get up and look for the circumstances they want, and, if they can't find them, they make them.'*
>
> —GEORGE BERNARD SHAW

I believed being a hands-on mom was the best gift anyone could give their children. So, I ensured being constantly available for my teen and her 8-year-old brother—from teaching them myself, helping them with their projects, preparing them for school events and cleaning their closets to ordering their favourite meals. Although there were no accolades for me in particular, I would often pat myself for doing a great job.

The smug mom got a wake-up call, quite literally. Once when I was indisposed at an assignment, I got a frantic call from my daughter asking me to order her a pizza as the cook hadn't turned up. And no amount of prodding to do it herself worked. Till then I'd never realized it was always her mother who helped her select a meal, get the best deal of the day or, say, call back the outlet to report on substandard quality. Recognizing my zealous overparenting, I consciously decided to take a step back to let the children find their way through. So now, whenever we order food or dine out, it's our son who plans the meal while our daughter places the order. Initially, there would always be more than what we could consume, but gradually she has become more judicious.

Parents seldom realize that in their ardour to do the best for their children, they end up micromanaging their lives.

Unfortunately, instead of having it easy, this makes the children's lives only difficult as they find themselves at a loss when they need to fend for themselves. Young people should actually be encouraged to develop independence early on. It needs to be a part of growing up as independence helps build their decision-making skills which they will need on a daily basis once they grow up to be adults.

Being able to take age-appropriate decisions on their own in turn builds their confidence and also resilience as they begin to learn through trial and error. When we give our children the freedom to experience life fully, they learn its many important lessons. 'Independence supports a young person's overall sense of well-being,' point out experts, which is why it's crucial for parents to work out a balance between supporting kids and encouraging them to become more independent at the same time.

Counter the Urge to Micromanage

Spiritual masters across the world emphasize that teaching children skill sets to earn their living is far better than leaving them pots of money. 'It's not what you do for your children, but what you teach them to do for themselves is what will give them a good life,' they say. One cannot agree more.

In our efforts to provide nothing but the very best to our kids, we have inadvertently turned into a breed of helicopter parents hovering over their children and leaping in before or at the slightest hint of discomfort, challenge or threat of failure. It may have innocently begun with scampering to collect goodies for their 'khoi bag' at kiddy birthday parties to helping around with school assignments in order to get top grades. It soon moves to fighting their battles in the playground or school to constant efforts at making their lives easier—from cleaning their closets to providing the latest gizmo. Sadly enough, it hardly makes their lives any easier.

Allow Them to Flourish

Renowned author and motivational speaker Dr Wayne Dyer in his book, *Change Your Thoughts, Change Your Life,* confides, whenever he stepped in to tell his children 'how', he encountered resistance. 'When I bite my tongue, zip my lips and retreat into silence, they not only figure it out themselves, but a calm energy replaces their frustration,' says Dyer. Fondly called 'the father of motivation', Dyer exhorts people to start living in a world which works far better with less meddling. Parents need to trust the inherent abilities of their children and allow them to flourish. And guess what? More, not less, seems to get accomplished.

I made an interesting observation over my visits to the swimming pool with my children during the summers. I noticed that children of anxious parents who clambered to the poolside at every cry of discomfort or pestered the coach to give more attention to their wards, actually took longer to learn swimming independently.

Our elders rightly believed that labour and struggle provide us with an inherent strength and wherewithal to handle the ups and downs of life. Remember the 'pupa story' wherein the baby butterfly struggled to come out of the tiny hole of the pupa by earnestly flapping its tiny, wet wings? When someone took pity and slit the hole wider to make it easier for the butterfly to emerge, it actually wriggled out and died. For, the flapping basically ensures the wings are strengthened and enables it to fly.

So when our kids seek autonomy, it does not amount to rebelliousness or disrespect. When we allow them the freedom to take age-appropriate decisions, it's like strengthening their wings to enable them a steady flight when they are adults.

Watch Out for the Pygmalion Effect

Children often develop traits based on how they are treated in their growing up years. While everyone is born with an inherent temperament, one acquires the ability to conduct oneself amicably over time. It's the surroundings, experiences and positive handling by parents and peers which shape the personalities. Parents are the main source of a child's self-worth. How people value themselves, behave with others, perform at school, achieve at work and relate in marriage—all stem from the strength of their self-image. That is to say, building a child's self-esteem is his passport to a lifetime of mental health and social happiness.

Namita*, an academic, is over-conscious about grooming her 16-year-old daughter well, to the point that she is constantly pulling her up for everything—from her laid-back attitude and dressing style to her weight. As a consequence of the mother's condescending attitude, the girl often finds herself lashing out at friends for no reason. Her erratic behaviour is only causing her to lose friends.

How we treat our children matters more than how they

behave. Noted educationist and counsellor Cedric M. Kenny calls it the Pygmalion Effect. We all know Pygmalion was a Greek sculptor who carved a statue of a beautiful woman that was subsequently brought to life. The essence of George Bernard Shaw's play *Pygmalion* (the basis for the musical hit *My Fair Lady*) is that one person, by his positive effort and will, can truly transform another person. In the play, Eliza Doolittle, the girl who was transformed from a plain flower girl to a fine lady, says: 'The difference between a lady and a flower girl is not how she behaves, but how she is treated.'

Kenny claims that parents play a Pygmalion-like role in developing able children and transforming their performance. While some treat kids in ways which bring out their best, others like Professor Higgins, Eliza's condescending tutor, perhaps unintentionally, treat them in a way which impedes their development.

Give Them Room to Grow

We were on a holiday in the hills of Darjeeling and Gangtok where we encountered two young girls (probably just out of their teens) from Mumbai. They showed pictures of the famed Changu Lake which they had visited despite heavy downpour and landslides. The two confided they were suckers for adventure holidays and regularly took three vacations a year, taking their elderly, but enthusiastic parents along. One couldn't help being impressed by their zest for life, affable nature and cool confidence as they shared how they planned each of their holidays with great precision. It was creditable on the part of their parents too for giving their girls leeway to follow their passions.[8]

When we allow our children to be themselves, follow their passions and lead a zesty life (of course with suitable guidance), we are sure to bring up confident and convivial human beings with an indomitable will.

A friend's daughter is a classic example of personal strength and conviction. Raunak, 20, studies in India while her parents live in the Middle East. Even though her parents remain connected with her through the day, the youngster manages practically everything on her own—from hopping between cities (to take exams), deciding on accommodations, booking tickets to even remembering to buy gifts for her domestic help on her trips back home. At the same time, there are people I know who are so overprotective about their youngsters that they do not even let them cross the road on their own. The damage being done to their personalities is often visible. They are likely to be more vulnerable to the challenges of life or become too judgemental of others with differing beliefs.

Ways to Foster Independence

Now, how does one make a youngster self-reliant—develop skills and resources to help him cope with extreme situations using his sense of judgement and problem-solving skills? Interestingly, independence is not something children can gain on their own—it is a gift to be given by the parents. We alone can provide kids the essential ingredients for gaining independence by:

---

[8]'Parenteen: Give your children leeway to grow'. 28 May 2016, Source: The Times of India Group. © BCCL. All Rights Reserved

- Giving them our love and respect
- Showing confidence in their abilities
- Balancing between guidance and freedom
- Teaching responsibility
- Encouraging exploration
- Listening to them with open minds

As a mother eager to bring up self-reliant children herself, I realize what is key: parents must counter the constant urge to be there and do everything for their kids. Grooming them to be self-sufficient by simple acts, say, cleaning their cupboards themselves or handling money, can go a long way in helping them stand on their own two feet. Children are bound to goof up several times, but letting them learn from their mistakes and generously praising a job well done will help build their self-esteem.

Powerful parents, who want their children to succeed, know it's important to be a strong support system for children, but they judiciously need to strike a balance between when to step in and step out in order to let them be.

8
Stay Informed and Set Boundaries

*'It's all right letting yourself go,
as long as you can get yourself back.'*

—MICK JAGGER

Giving our children space and desisting from micromanaging their lives are definitely traits of sensible parenting. But, it certainly does not mean letting youngsters do whatever they please or losing track of their lives, all in the name of independence.

- A bunch of young terrorists, all barely out of their teens, hacked innocent people in an upmarket eatery in Bangladesh even as they smiled and chatted with each other. Far from hailing from impoverished backgrounds, these terrorists came from well-to-do families, had passed out from an upscale school in Dhaka and were enrolled in universities abroad. Unfortunately, their parents were clueless about their fatal escapade. (1 July 2016)[9]
- A software engineer of a renowned multinational in Chennai was ruthlessly killed by a stalker, an engineering graduate himself. Even though the girl had mentioned being stalked to a colleague, once again, her parents were

---

[9]'Dhaka: "Normal, regular guys" who carried out Bangladesh terror attack', *CNN*, 4 July 2016, https://edition.cnn.com/2016/07/04/asia/bangladesh-attackers-isis/index.html?no-st=1517462234

clueless about their daughter's ordeal. (24 June 2016)[10]
- The number of suicides in Kota (known as an education hub) in Rajasthan by disgruntled students is a matter of grave concern. As one loses count of the number of young boys and girls who succumb to the pressures of competitions in that city, what is distressing is the complete disconnect of some parents with the anxieties of their youngsters.[11]

A bizarre fallout of the modern world is this lack of substantial communication between the parents and children. This could be either due to overindulgence, wherein parents have no idea what their children are up to, or the overbearing attitude of parents which unwittingly creates a communication barrier. As a result, children are unable to share their discomfiture and anxieties with them.

Even as the father of one of the teenaged terrorists (of the Dhaka attack) apologized for the gruesome killings, he revealed that his son had gone missing a few months back. He pleaded he had no idea that his son, who was a brilliant student, a footballer and a Manchester United enthusiast, had

---

[10]'Infosys employee hacked to death by "stalker" at Chennai railway station', *Hindustan Times*, 24 June 2016, http://www.hindustantimes.com/india-news/infosys-employee-hacked-to-death-by-stalker-at-chennai-railway-station/story-YHcb7PeP4D4uLhqSlUy6oN.html

[11]Charu Bahri, 'Kota's student suicides: Parents, don't stress your kids or impose your dreams on them', FirstPost, 15 April 2017, http://www.firstpost.com/india/kotas-student-suicides-parents-dont-stress-your-kids-or-impose-your-dreams-on-them-3386080.html

been radicalized. Meanwhile, parents of children who commit suicide are also often at a loss as to what caused them to end their lives.

Parents are not just providers of necessities and comforts for their children; they must also seek to know what ails their minds—what keeps them brooding awake in the nights, who is encroaching their zones of privacy and security or who is brainwashing them with radical ideas. It's all right to grant youngsters their personal space, but it is wise to keep track of their friends and acquaintances or who they repeatedly interact with. Being able to read their body language and quickly register changes in behaviour, too, go a long way in helping us anticipate signs of depression, aggression or disenchantment and act upon them in time.[12]

Boundaries are Essential

Besides being sensibly and necessarily clued on to the lives of children, it is equally important to outline certain boundaries for them. Everyone needs rules or else there would be utter chaos—imagine if there were no traffic rules, there would be a complete gridlock. Just like rules help us organize our activities and enable us to do our jobs well, similarly, setting clear boundaries for our children help to keep them on the right track.

Most kids think parents are being unreasonable when they clamp down time limits on their freedom to talk on the phone, use the Internet, party with friends or follow a deadline to be

---

[12] 'Parenteen: Stay clued to your kid's life', 9 July 2016. Source: The Times of India Group. © BCCL. All Rights Reserved

home. Although parents need not bog down the children with excessive dos and don'ts, effective parenting requires forewarning kids and outlining certain basic norms to be followed. Time embargo, for instance, is one boundary which inculcates a sense of discipline in children, besides ensuring their safety.

'Setting consistent boundaries for your children is very important,' said early intervention specialist Jane Krill Thomson at a parenting workshop in Kolkata which I attended. 'You are not breaking their spirit by setting those limitations, but helping them channelize their energies,' she claimed. Just as a harness prevents climbers from falling off the cliff, consistent boundaries act as a buffer for children to explore, learn and climb, felt the American expert, who was in India serving a tenure as the then Consul General's wife.

Thomson candidly shared how as parents of two teenage girls, both she and her spouse had to handle constant conflict for the boundaries that they set. For instance, she insisted on being informed about their whereabouts by her children and demanded basic etiquettes with guests and elders. Sitting in the audience, I was pleasantly surprised at how the concerns and challenges of parents across continents and cultures remained more or less identical.

Counsellors and psychologists across the board—whether Thomson or Prakash—agree that defining boundaries work well for children, including teenagers. In fact, they tend to feel safer when they have clear limitations before them. For instance, having clear time embargos serve the dual purpose of instilling a sense of responsibility towards time as well as a sense of accountability towards parents. Teens, in particular, have enough changes to deal with in their lives, having parents clearly define the playing field tends to provide a vital degree of certainty and stability, they say.

Moreover, having boundaries teaches responsibility—that actions have consequences. We have to make our children see that rules are a fact of life. Just like there are rules for traffic, schools and colleges, there are rules of friendship, family and society too—that certain things are unacceptable. And as you face the music from the principal for breaking rules in schools, when you cross the boundaries of agreeable behaviour as a friend, as a citizen and a human being, you have to face the repercussions. Quite understandably, children, who are brought up with no restrictions on behaviour, are bound to get confused when faced with restrictions of life and society as adults. That explains why some children, who are brought up amid complete lack of restrictions and total indulgence, grow up to believe they own the world and frequently indulge in all kinds of nefarious activities with impudence.

Be Ready to Face Conflict

Setting boundaries does not mean restricting the children from doing everything they want to. It simply means saying yes and no. Just like a door which sometimes needs to be opened, sometimes closed or left ajar depending on the requirement, parents too must know when to relax or tighten the restrictions.

Be firm but fair, recommends Kenny in his book, *Love Without Spoiling, Discipline Without Nagging*. 'Relax your rules bit by bit as your child displays more maturity. If he or she can't handle the freedom, tighten the reins and try again in a few months,' he suggests.

Laying down rules for the teens to follow is a daunting task that all parents grapple with at home, often leading them on a guilt trip. Add to that a natural tendency of teens to despise and defy restrictions that are imposed on them and there's ample ammunition for a parenting predicament.

But, conflict arises when your values clash with those of your teens who may be under the influence of social media and friends. 'All my friends go to pubs and discos or indulge in mall hopping on weekends, but I'm never allowed,' moans Rachita*, 15. 'I feel so deprived and often have a showdown with my mom,' she confesses. Her mother, a media professional, is firm about her decision, but does indulge her teen every once in a while by taking her out along with some of her friends.

When we are consistently fair and do not hesitate to speak our truths with the children, they eventually begin to respect our decisions. However, setting too many boundaries cause resentment, so we must choose our rules judiciously. But no matter how difficult your battles with teens may be, know they are vital. Says an interesting Chinese proverb—Parents, who do not put down their foot, have children stepping on their toes.

Explain Your Decisions

When boundaries are violated, there has to be consequences and when consequences are agreed upon by the teen while setting the boundary, it is helpful in reducing the heartburn.

Banker and single mother, Kavita* has a fixed time embargo of 6 p.m. for her 16-year-old daughter, who like others her age, loves to hang out with friends. But the youngster clearly knows any violation of the embargo means being grounded for an entire month. Since teenagers are quite adept at reasoning unlike smaller children, it's always better to explain the reasons behind your decisions instead of merely saying, 'Because I said so'. Even while laying out the margins of conduct, it's a good idea to involve the youngsters, make them see reason and take into account their opinion so you have a jointly agreed upon code of conduct, suggest counsellors. This way, they would be more motivated to adhere, than if they were merely hammered upon.

Couple It With Love

Even as parents set rules and limitations for our children, we clearly need to demonstrate that we live within reasonable boundaries ourselves. We cannot afford to ask them to merely 'do as we say and not do it ourselves'. Moreover, it is important not to behave like their adversaries or make them feel as if we are always out to spoil their fun. Let them know you are on the same side by frequently expressing love even as you exhort them to adhere to your boundaries. Make them feel secure in your love.

Confrontations aren't uncommon even in our household; I've come to realize they are part of teen parenting. But following such episodes are instances where affection is aplenty, which I think helps drive home my point eventually.

9

Equip Them to Recognize and Fight Predators

> *'Although the world is full of suffering,
> it is also full of the overcoming of it.'*
>
> —HELEN KELLER

'I will never bring a child into this world. It's such a scary, dirty place that I cannot imagine my daughter or son out on their own alone,' a journalist friend once commented while chatting over coffee. I was unable to understand the sentiment behind this statement coming from a seasoned scribe married for several years. Revelling in the bliss of having just been blessed with our bundle of joy, I failed to comprehend his concerns then.

Today, as one scans newspapers, flicks channels or matches notes with friends and parents, one understands the looming magnitude of the insecurity children face daily—be it on the streets, schools, colleges, malls or markets, public transport or in some cases even within the seemingly safe confines of our homes. Predators seem to be prowling around practically everywhere in the guise of cabbies, conductors, peons, teachers and uncles.

Every time we come across an incident of child abuse or molestation one experiences mixed emotions of embarrassment, revulsion and anger. But for a parent, it means added fear and apprehension for his/her child's safety. The uncanny rise in such incidents across the world in the last few years is a cause of great concern to parents, police and psychologists. The grim situation demands us to equip our children adequately in our war against these ignoble elements.[13]

Recognize Predators and Fortify Kids

In order to ensure the safety of children, it is important to understand the dynamics of child sexual abuse and believe we have the power to protect them. To begin with, know that molesters are people who stalk and hunt our children. They are smart and cunning people, often trusted individuals like relatives, teachers, coaches, friends or caregivers, and one would hardly expect them to commit such crimes.

As someone who is fastidious about the safety and security of kids, not just my own, but every child on this planet, I recommend all parents should compulsorily have a frank and effective communication system at home. They must teach their children, young ones or teens, to be alert and on their guard all the time. Help them identify a bad touch, an uncomfortably lingering handshake or any other inappropriate gesture of friends, relatives or strangers. And most importantly, be brave enough to express their dissent immediately, for silence is often taken as approval.

Curb Information Leak

Sitting in the train once, I came across a couple of young girls, who were on their way to Kolkata from Patna. Evidently, the friends were meeting after a holiday and had a lot to share with

---

[13]'Parenteen: Brace them to combat predators', 26 September 2015. Source: The Times of India Group. © BCCL. All Rights Reserved

each other. An hour into the journey, and everybody within earshot knew where they lived, where they studied or stayed as paying guests and umpteen other personal details. I noticed a middle-aged passenger with a fixed gaze on the unmindful girls. When the two lay down for the night still chatting animatedly on their upper berths, the guy audaciously stood up to catch a better glimpse. Desperate to draw the attention of the girls, I blurted, 'Sir, is your luggage up there with them?' pointing towards the girls' berths. 'No, no I'm just stretching my limbs,' he said visibly embarrassed to the amusement of other passengers who too had noticed his misdemeanour.

Youngsters seem to live in their own world, often oblivious of the people around and the dangers related to them. I remember as young kids we were always warned against sharing personal details with strangers unless lost in a crowd. But today, when youngsters meet and chat in public, one usually notices they are blissfully unaware of their surroundings and the possibility of unsavoury elements watching out for prey. Being watchful of our behaviour and conversations with friends or while on the phone around people is something we need to groom our teens about.

Ensure Internet Safety

The Internet is another major source of personal information giveaway. Children (not denying a substantial number of adults too!) believe in liberally uploading not just explicit pictures, but even details about their romantic status, where they holiday, what they shop or what they eat on social networking sites. The latest mantra is, what's the point in having fun if you don't flaunt it to the world! However, in all of this, what one forgets is that criminals scour the Internet for details on potential victims, and that this information can be misused in a big way. The phenomenon clearly explains the reason behind the sudden spurt in cases of Internet stalking and cybercrimes; these have now become a major concern to both parents and police.

'Sharing of thoughts and expressions on the Internet is beneficial for children in shaping their personalities,' feels psychotherapist Nilima Kumar. But, too much information tends to be revealed, often inadvertently, which is proving to be hazardous, concedes the senior counsellor at a Birla Foundation school.

Every parent must compulsorily have Internet safety chat with children, warning them of the hazards that are lurking therein. Some might roll their eyes impatiently claiming to be already aware of all this, but there is no harm in checking with them every once in a while.

> **Irrespective of age or sex, it is crucial to follow some important rules for Internet safety**
>
> **Passwords are private:** Do not share your password even with friends. Although hard to imagine, friendships change and you never know when people can become angry and malicious.
>
> **Check your privacy settings:** Everyone needs to be careful about what one reveals and expresses on a public platform. In most cases, the default privacy settings will give your posts maximum public exposure which can be very dangerous. The best settings are where only friends can see what you post as the 'Friends of Friends' setting can leave you exposed and vulnerable.

Equip Them to Recognize and Fight Predators

Be cautious of friend requests: Play it safe and only accept friend requests from friends in the real world. Fake profiles are also created for cyber bullying. Whenever a new friend request comes in, be sure to check the person's profile first and see if anything looks fishy.

Think before you post: Limit personal contact information in your profile and posts. Never give away your phone number or address. Even though you can delete something (a post, picture or comment), you can never permanently erase something that has been published on the Internet.

Disable location services: Avoid announcing your holidays and wait to post your vacation pictures only when you are back as you only make yourself vulnerable to unscrupulous elements scouring for information.

Be wary of online acquaintances: Never agree to meet online friends without informing parents. Do not share personal information or share pictures and videos with strangers. Thirty-two per cent of teens have been contacted online by a complete stranger, say Amanda Lenhart and Mary Madden in their 2007 report 'Friendship, Strangers and Safety in Online Social Networks'. Profile-owning teens are much more likely to be contacted.

Blogging is public: Many teens find blogging an easy and interesting way to express or be updated about each other's thoughts and feelings. But your teenager needs to know that anyone can view these blogs, so their information really isn't private like a personal handwritten journal. As they bare their personal thoughts to complete strangers they can be used to their disadvantage.

Online romance mostly spells trouble: Unfortunately, many youngsters do not realize that anyone can hide behind a computer. That is why, it is important that you talk to your child about the dangers of starting an online romance.

Listen to Them

Unfortunately, only one in five kids who have been sexually abused, will report it, say experts. So, the single most effective tool in the fight against molesters is having frequent frank conversations with children. Doing away with inhibitions and talking about the issue freely with kids in an age-appropriate manner will go a long way in protecting them, claims Nilima Kumar. 'Parents and teachers must work to build a comfort level with children in order to win their confidence so they can discuss any incident that makes them uncomfortable,' she says.

Once in a while, catch a calm and peaceful moment with your teen to casually ask, 'Is there anything you want to tell me, anything which has been bothering you?' Listen intently to the answers. It is sensible parenting to avoid scolding at that moment even if the child shares something negative. Be very clear with your kids that no matter what they do, they should never keep secrets about their problems from you.

Be the Rock of Gibraltar

'Recognizing the red flags is equally important. These could be changes in the body language of your kid, sudden dipping of academic performance, physical and behavioural symptoms like aggressive behaviour, crying or withdrawing into a shell,' points out Patna-based clinical psychologist and psychotherapist Binda Singh. 'Not believing your child when he/she shares a disconcerting fact about any violation can be very damaging, often leading to psychosomatic disorders,' she adds.[14]

An important thing is to trust and believe your child. Parents and peers of victims often tend to berate them either for their dressing sense or carefree behaviour bringing this misdemeanour upon them. What kids need, first and foremost, is a sympathetic ear and your conviction that you will stand behind them like the Rock of Gibraltar.

Sheelta Kumar, a Delhi-based schoolteacher, recommends parents to avoid reacting aggressively when informed of a violation by kids. Getting hysterical, disbelieving or fixing the blame only adds to their trauma, making them feel guilty. What needs to be reinforced is that it is never a child's fault when someone mistreats him/her. If victimized, it is never something he/she should be ashamed of or hide from his/her parents.

Parents must ensure their children get this message, 'Even if you have made a mistake, I will help you and continue to love you'. Fear and anger of parents should not deter them from seeking help of adults. Tell them they must confide in you about anyone who makes them uncomfortable, verbally or physically, even if the person happens to be a close relative or friend.

And, last but not least, it's crucial to develop a ready strategy to encounter all kinds of devious situations. It could comprise keeping emergency numbers on their speed dial, carrying pepper spray, training them to physically defend themselves and in extreme circumstances exercising their vocal chords to

---

[14]'Never a child's fault if molested by predator', 10 February 2016. Source: The Times of India Group. © BCCL. All Rights Reserved

the maximum and kicking where it hurts the most.

If at all one comes to know of a situation of physical violation at home, a friend's home or place of education, it's crucial to immediately swing into action—collate facts, organize and take up the issue with the authorities concerned.

To sum it up, parents need to talk, teach, listen and, above all, watch over their children to ward off predators. Cool confidence, firm behaviour and determination to bring violators to book should be every parent's moral duty to imbue in children as a bulwark for a safe existence in this world of predators.

10
Instil the Humility to Apologize and Seek Forgiveness

*'The more we know the better we forgive.
Whoever feels deeply, feels for all who live.'*

—GERMAINE DE STAËL

In my career as a journalist spanning over two decades, I happened to interview an array of people from diverse fields, but never interacted with a spiritual master. So, while writing this book, an occasion of a one-to-one interface with Anandmurti Gurumaa, a contemporary mystic known for her pragmatic wisdom and teachings, was not just unique, but insightful.

In the course of our discussion on ways of effective parenting of youngsters, I took the liberty of asking something about the Ramayana which often needled my mind. I queried: 'What lesson should one draw from Lord Rama's act of abandoning his devoted wife Sita and sending her to the jungle when she needed him the most?' The spiritual leader, known for her eloquent and witty discourses, said in her inimitable style: 'Although we revere him as God, we must not forget Rama took birth as a human being who is, after all, prone to errors. Valmiki's Ramayana, towards the end, clearly mentions that Lord Rama realized his mistake and apologized profusely to Goddess Sita for his grave error.'

I returned home mulling over what the spiritual leader had shared. If someone as revered and sacred as Lord Rama could own up his error of judgement and apologize, what prevents us, lesser mortals from doing the same? This was probably the lesson that he was trying to get across to humanity through

Instil the Humility to Apologize and Seek Forgiveness

his act—no matter how great, powerful or knowledgeable you may be, you are liable to make mistakes. But, you must possess the humility to acknowledge it and seek forgiveness from the person wronged.

Unfortunately, in reality, the older, richer and more powerful we get, the more averse we are to acknowledge our errors, leave aside apologizing for them. Children, who grow up noticing this disdain for acknowledging mistakes by elders around them, are bound to be just as irreverent as their seniors. How often we tend to hurt each other at home, work or social gatherings, sometimes inadvertently. At times, even when we realize we have erred, it's difficult to acknowledge the mistake and make up for it as ego stands in the way of saying a heartfelt sorry. We increasingly come across family members, relatives and best friends, who refuse to talk to each other for years, following a petty argument, just because neither side wants to be the first to let go of their pride and break the ice. This is primarily because right since childhood they have come to construe apologizing as a sign of weakness. But, on the contrary, looking oneself in the eye and standing tall to own up to one's mistakes actually demonstrates a great strength of character.

Begin With Yourself

As parents, we sometimes make parenting blunders, but may not possess the gumption to own up and apologize to our kids. Children, for instance, often point out they tend to be at the receiving end of temper flare-ups of their parents or teachers if they have had a hard day at work or a tough time in the house with their spouses or the domestic help. But, both parents and teachers seldom display the sensitivity to recognize and apologize for their lapse.

Apologies need to be modelled. As parents, we need to be willing to say sorry to others in front of our children and to them too when required. We cannot expect youngsters to be introspective and repentant of inappropriate behaviour when we set a poor example of being egoistic and arrogant ourselves.

'How come you took so long to dress yet your hair is looking so unruly? Now, hurry up and fix it up quickly,' I once blurted without thinking as soon as our daughter walked in, seeking comments, dressed in her new lehenga. We were attending a family wedding in another city. I bit my tongue almost instantly as I saw the damage done by that candid comment—for her smiling eyes instantly turned sad, angry, hurt and defiant. Obviously, I had erred. In my tearing hurry to leave on time, I had overlooked my teen's efforts at dressing up painstakingly in the traditional attire, despite all her unease.

I salvaged the evening by convincing her she looked 'special' and that I didn't mean to hurt her self-confidence. We eventually made up and went on to have a great time together at the wedding. I realized how a careless comment and a parent's ego could have turned into a spoiler for a perfect evening.

Parents need to know that when they say sorry to children, it has a threefold impact. To begin with, it immediately makes them feel better, strengthens the relationship with the kids, and most importantly teaches them the crucial lesson of the need to own up and apologize no matter how young or old, weak or powerful they may be.

Why Apologizing is Important

In today's world of rising competition and conflict, it's vital to acquire the ability to recognize our own mistakes and also ensure that our children are imbued with that quality. Since no one is perfect, we are bound to do something to hurt another person at some point in our lives.

Come to think of it, why is an apology so important? Believe it or not, there have been scientific studies on the power of apologizing. Both psychologists and spiritual masters agree that apologizing is crucial as it heals both sides. It acts as a balm by reducing the hurt as well as the guilt. And this ability to recognize mistakes and say sorry should be inculcated in children early on. For, when a child learns how to say sorry, he gains more than a social skill. He also learns how to undo his mistakes, take responsibility for his actions and be considerate about other people's feelings.

In a world of high aggression and brashness, most children grow up giving apology a complete miss, unless compelled. Class IX student Swastik Panda points out that boys in his class almost never bother to apologize to each other, but feel compulsorily inclined to do so to teachers or those in authority. Although Swastik claims to say sorry once in a while when the situation cannot be salvaged otherwise, his friend Siddhant Patnaik confesses he has no qualms in apologizing at all. 'Whenever I realize I have overstepped my boundaries, be it with friends or family, I do not mind saying sorry,' he says. It is probably because we are not averse to saying sorry to each other at home, Siddhant explains.

What It Means

While an apology does tend to curb the negative impact of any deed, at the same time mere mumbling one without any genuine feeling has no meaning. What one means by saying sorry is that the offending behaviour will not be repeated. But, only we know as parents, how untrue it can sometimes be. For, children more often than not use 'sorry' as a free ticket out of trouble.

So, what parents need to do is emphasize that apologies are meaningless, unless you change the offending behaviour, else the same offence will keep getting committed. This kind of counterfeit atonement is often evident in unrepentant terrorists, hardened criminals and even celebrities, who only tend to repeat offences with impunity the moment they are out on their own, as they are unwilling to change.

Meanwhile, an honest apology should never be followed up with excuses, for instance: 'I am sorry I hit you, but hey, you made me angry'. Besides, instead of a generic sorry, it should necessarily be specific referring to the act with, 'I will make sure that what I did will never happen again'.

No Point Forcing It

Experts caution parents to hate the act, not the kid. And it's advisable not to force a sorry upon children. 'If the apology is not sincere or blurted just to get out of a sticky situation, it is meaningless,' points out Nandini Choudhury Brahmachari. If the child refuses to apologize, she recommends leaving it for the moment and approaching the issue later on, instead of making a furore about it then.

Instil the Humility to Apologize and Seek Forgiveness

The fact is when we force children to apologize in the heat of the moment, we might feel we have done the job of active parenting well, but it is unlikely to help children truly understand the effects of their misbehaviour. Even psychologists recommend postponing the apology when everyone is calm and collected, instead of forcing it when tempers are flaring. This might lead to a considerably more sincere 'sorry'. And the youngsters will understand, take responsibility of their actions better and develop the empathy needed to learn from mistakes.

Forgiveness Goes Hand in Hand

Even as we teach children to acknowledge their mistakes, atone for them and make amends, we must also model the attribute of forgiveness. When we realize and acknowledge the other person's perspective in committing the 'wrong', it reduces the negativity. The best gift we can give ourselves and to our children is to delete a negative or sad incident and refuse to keep going back to it. When a teen musters the courage to confess a mistake, remaining calm and positive will go a long way in helping him become an honest and confident individual.

Media professional Sonali Rai* confides she had to gather her wits to remain calm when her 16-year-old son confessed having alcohol at his friend's place. 'Although I don't like hearing that you took alcohol, I forgive you this once because I appreciate you had the courage to own up,' she told her visibly repentant son. By controlling her outburst and forgiving her son, Sonali underlined both the integrity of character as well as the need to give people another chance.

As we train children to let go of their pain or hurt, accept a well-meaning apology and move on, we groom them in an important skill which will hold them in good stead in life as adults. Be sure we are also paving the way for a safer society as youngsters, who carry their childhood pains, anger and grouses, sometimes go on to perpetuate all kinds of atrocities on people through violence and homicide.

11

Spare the Rod and Know Your Child

'If you judge people, you have no time to love them.'

—MOTHER TERESA

Most of us have grown up hearing the old adage of sparing the rod and spoiling the child. As children, we might have been punished for our mistakes physically, say, with a slap or two by parents or even teachers at school. It might have worked back then. But, let me categorically state that corporal punishments do not work now, with this generation of children. Times have changed phenomenally and our children operate in a totally new world, with varied mindsets and compulsions. So, raising our hands on kids, particularly teens to make our point or to pull them up for their mistakes, is definitely a bad idea and should be completely avoided.

A cross section of parents, counsellors, psychiatrists and cops I interacted with only endorsed the fact that physical punishments tend to be counterproductive and defeat their very purpose. With a virtual explosion of communication in the last ten years, as parents, we need to acknowledge that we cannot apply the same parenting methods that our elders adopted in bringing us up.

Desist Hurting Your Child

Adults usually hit children when they feel they have lost control of the situation, are in a hurry to impose decisions or averse to spending time to deal with the circumstances more sensitively. Shouting, ranting, slapping or locking up the child is actually opposed to the spirit of discipline, maintains motivator Cedric M. Kenny. In order to discipline children, we first need to be self-disciplined and in control of our own emotions and faculties, he writes in his book, *Love Without Spoiling, Discipline Without Nagging*. According to child psychiatrist J. Gary, 'It is usually a weak parent or teacher, who administers corporal punishment, because that person wants to exercise control over the child by inflicting pain.'

Ohio, USA-based academic Suparna Basu, raising two boys aged 10 and 19, too believes corporal punishment should be an absolute no. 'I strongly believe [that] no situation calls for any sort of punishment which causes physical and emotional pain. Each time we hit a child, it emboldens him until a point is reached when he or she won't care. And to push him to that point only defeats the purpose of discipline,' she states. With young adult children, one must be especially careful not to escalate the situation as growing kids with rushing hormones cannot control their anger very well and can retaliate easily without a warning. The recent bizarre incident (9 December 2017) of a young boy in Delhi who slaughtered his mother and sister for snatching away his mobile phone is only a case in point.[15]

Not just physical, but any kind of punishment for that matter, has lost its relevance in this high-tech age of communication, feels Nishith Kumar, a father of three young children from Pune. Parents only need to counsel and apprise

---

[15] '15-year-old Greater Noida boy confesses to killing mother, sister', *The Tribune*, 9 December 2017, http://www.tribuneindia.com/news/nation/15-year-old-greater-noida-boy-confesses-to-killing-mother-sister/510639.html

children of the consequences of various situations. 'We can only explain the "why" in detail so as to equip our kids to take an informed decision. Punishments do not work on this new breed,' he says.

Navika Khanna*, on the other hand, confesses to often being driven to a point where she's forced to thrash her teenage daughter when she simply refuses to sit down to study or put away her iPad. But, invariably after such incidents, Khanna claims to feel more miserable than her daughter. 'No mother likes to hit her child, but I can't merely sit and watch her waste away her crucial time,' she says with a wry smile.

Perhaps, Khanna would have done better to first introspect her actions about indulging her child ever so often for the wrong reasons, before losing her control at the teen's growing obsessions. Physical punishments never end up solving problems. We can hope for long-term solutions only when we take out time to logically explain to the teens the right and the wrong and justify our rules and decisions.

Meanwhile, cops as well as psychiatrists trace the roots of juvenile criminals to childhood violence as both categorically agree that violence only begets violence. Even the dynamic spiritual leader, Swami Vivekananda observed more than a century ago: 'Physical punishments only make a child ruder, more aggressive and inconsiderate.'

Are Punishments Totally Outmoded?

Although one needs to rule out punishments that inflict emotional and physical pain on children, the crucial question is how to control their misdemeanours and repeated wrongs.

Is the concept of punishments totally outmoded for this generation of children?

Punishments, as a form of correction and discipline for children and young adults, can never go obsolete. But, in this age of spiralling development of science and technology coupled with high-speed evolution of our children's minds, we need to alter the orientation of punishment and try out differential reinforcements for positive behaviour. Both parents and educators must realize when they are correcting children that they have a dual role to play—of a referee as well as a coach. While the referee identifies a foul and blows his whistle, the coach patiently trains the student to correct a mistake while upholding his/her self-esteem and dignity.[16]

Check Out Alternate Solutions

Every parent brings up his/her child with certain morals outlining the norms of behaviour. Now, these rules, which are usually never questioned or violated when they are small children, may suddenly appear constricting to them as youngsters. As a result, one can expect arguments and violations of varying degrees, depending on each one's temperament. It is imperative for parents to have an open discussion at the outset with kids about their rights and privileges and circumstances which can cause their withdrawal.

Deprivation: If a youngster continues to commit the same error, despite repeated warnings, or commits a serious misdeed, depriving or taking away of facilities or a gadget he holds dear

---

[16]See Cedric M. Kenny, *Love Without Spoiling, Discipline Without Nagging*.

can be an effective tool of enforcing positive behaviour. For instance, you can take away the cell phone, iPod or iPad, if despite warnings your kid's academic performance continues to dip due to spending excessive time on his favourite gadget.

Although some kids might feign indifference when you remove a privilege, be assured it does affect them. It's just that they do not want us to know and feel empowered. Parents need to know their children well to withdraw the privilege that matters most to them, but return it once they make suitable amends.

Grounding or loss of social freedom: This can be yet another important tool. To most adolescents, freedom is the breath of life, so denying it can really hurt. Says Hyderabad-based Amrita Kaur, a working mother of a 19-year-old: 'Although I'm very friendly and indulgent with my daughter and believe she keeps no secrets from me, I have a definite set of restrictions in place which she knows can't be breached. She's aware she will have to pay in terms of losing out on her precious freedom.'

Ensure Solutions Don't Backfire

Even as you adopt various tools to enforce corrective behaviour, make sure you do not go overboard with your restrictions.

- Specify your time of withdrawal of benefits. For instance, take away the cell phone till your child brings back decent grades in exams. Withdrawal or confiscation of benefits is bound to cause sulking, so keep it task-specific and time-specific.
- Do not take away all freedoms or gadgets when you

are already grounding them from going out with friends. Remember your target is to temporarily reduce their freedom, not break their spirit. If you take away everything, then maybe they will have nothing to lose which just as well might induce more wayward behaviour.

- Do not stunt their growth as a form of punishment like forcing the teen to discontinue with his/her swimming/tennis lessons when training for an event. (Mary Kom's dad once burnt her gloves before a tournament.) This will only set them back socially, leading to a greater negative impact on their minds than anyone can imagine.

- Never keep bringing up past instances of misbehaviour or violations. Teens often complain that parents never forget the wrongs they commit and keep bringing them up. This riles them up even as they find themselves unwittingly repeating the mistakes and blunders. While the parents' intention of reminding the children may have been to caution, but the energy created is that of constant criticism.

- Corrections should never be an attack on the youngster's character and personality, for example: 'You always do stupid things'. Give a feedback on the mistake, not the child. Parents should never use harsh words on children, for they stay with them through life, says spiritual master Anandmurti Gurumaa. Be specific about evaluating mistakes and always explain the reason behind punishments.

- It is important for parents to keep in mind that punishments should never be sadistic. One needs to prove a point and most certainly leave a window open for meaningful communication.

Our goal is to improve behaviour and encourage our youngsters to take age-appropriate decisions. Using consequences and privileges are simply means of motivation to help them grow up to be responsible and emotionally strong adults.

Even as you use consequences and privileges (punishment and reward) as effective tools to discipline, do not expect changes in the child overnight. Like any new skill, better behaviour needs practice. When implementing a new consequence, you can expect some failure. Focus on knowing your child. You may need to restart a couple of times. If he behaves inappropriately repeatedly everywhere, your tools will take a while longer. Do not be disheartened, look for windows of good behaviour, appreciate and capitalize on them. Besides, never lose out on the opportunity to recognize his/her positive behaviour. For example, when you notice how your teen manages to control his otherwise volatile temper in front of guests despite extreme provocation by his sibling, remember to appreciate the trait later.

Parents need to realize every teen is unique, so the best disciplining tool for one may not be the same for another. We have to keep finding ways to break through the walls they put up to get them talking, learning and improving.

The bottom line is to remember positive parenting is not about raising a flock of obedient sheep, but raising dynamic people who shine through their lives.

12

Hold Your Horses When Mistakes Happen

> *'We should be careful to get out of an experience
> only the wisdom that is in it...'*
>
> —MARK TWAIN

Ragini was an extremely cheerful and boisterous girl, who was in school with me in Class X. Unable to control her giggles, she would always be pulled up by teachers in school and even at my mother's music school which she attended on weekends. But, for us youngsters, she was the one who used to break the monotony, whether of learning math or music.

One Saturday, she didn't turn up for the music class. As we began without her, mother got the appalling news—Ragini was no more. She had committed suicide that afternoon. While everyone from the music class rushed to her house, unable to immediately comprehend what had transpired, I remember withdrawing to my room.

The reason leading to the fatal decision by an otherwise happy teen seemed so flimsy that people refused to believe it. Ragini had apparently taken money to deposit the school fees which she dropped somewhere. When her parents chided her for it, she did not show any major distress, but asked to be left alone supposedly to finish her studies.

My adolescent years, thereafter, were spent wondering what could possibly have been going on in Ragini's mind that afternoon, what was it that had pulled the steam out of a vivacious girl and what if someone had entered the room at that moment and managed to change the course of events—she would be alive and giggling amid all of us. After the incident, I could sense the undercurrent of concern and apprehensions in my parents' behaviour with me.

Almost three decades later, I still have those questions raging in my mind every time I hear about a suicide by a youngster. The difference is now I can understand the pain and shock of the parents too. In most cases, the reasons leading to such fatal incidents are so inconsequential, they only leave the loved ones regretting the moment, wishing they could have handled the situation otherwise.

Stand By Your Child

Mistakes, big or small, keep getting committed by children. Why only them, we all make mistakes, wittingly or unwittingly. We may feel terrible about them, but the consequences of our deeds often double our pain. Most adults forget that children or teenagers are also like them. They usually know when they have erred and experience a dichotomy of emotions ranging from embarrassment, guilt and unhappiness to fear—what would their parents say or what would people think?

When mistakes happen, it is best to drop every other thought on your mind and focus on your child. **Let him know you are there for him, no matter what.** As adults, we are in a better position to put things in perspective, analyse situations and come up with solutions. No matter how intelligent or tech-savvy our youngsters may be, the fact is they have an immature brain. Scientists point out that while the amygdala, the area that controls fear and aggression, develops early, growth of the frontal cortex responsible for reasoning and self-control continues until early adulthood.

So adults, in general, and parents, in particular, must know how important it is to support our teens. Although it may be easier standing by them when they do something phenomenal, it is in times when they struggle or make a mistake that children need the maximum care.

Pop singer Ben E. King's song 'Stand by Me' of the 1960s couldn't be more relevant here to emphasize that we need to stand by our children.

When the night has come
And the land is dark
And the moon is the only light...
...I won't be afraid...
Just as long as you...stand by me

People all over acknowledge the importance of support during arduous times. Small wonder this song has suffused all cultures across continents since its release in 1961 (more than 400 artists have recorded versions of 'Stand by Me').

Today, it is imperative for not just parents, but all adults (teachers, trainers, friends, relatives or neighbours) to join forces in preventing our children from falling over the edge. For youngsters, ending their own lives seems to have become an increasingly easier option than sticking on to face difficult circumstances. We must emphasize that committing suicide does not relieve them of pain or suffering. On the contrary, they will consign themselves to bigger pain, greater suffering and longer strife. Just as any work that one ignores to do only becomes bigger and more complicated with time, troubles we refuse to confront now, will only get magnified eventually.

Condemn the Wrong

Being supportive of children, however, does not mean excusing their wrongful behaviour. It's true we need to berate the act, not the kids. But, parents must be careful not to encourage or cover up the wrong committed by them. Sometimes, overindulgent or overprotective parents refuse to take cognizance of the mistakes made by children and prefer to gloss over the problem. Some guardians take offence at being pointed out that their wards are indulging in unscrupulous behaviour at school, like being violent, cheating, stalking girls or passing lewd remarks, point out teachers. Indifference or overindulgence by guardians only tends to compound problems which could have been nipped in the bud, puts forth Aarti Sharma, student coordinator and administrator of a reputed school in Patna. 'We are often shocked by the aggression of parents, who are called when their children repeatedly violate the decorum of the school. They refuse to accept their kids' mistakes, leave aside discussing ways to amend the behaviour,' says Sharma.

When we keep rescuing our children from their mistakes, it's a double whammy for their personality growth. On the one hand, it makes them unsure about themselves as they always look for someone to help them out. On the other hand, they develop the impudence for crime, knowing they have their parents to bail them out of any mess. For instance, in the numerous car crashes by spoilt, carousing sons of the affluent class in India, the parents leave no stone unturned in distorting facts to save their children.

It is rightly said that in childhood, which is the age of dependence, a conscientious parent is often the best teacher. And, in adolescence or the age of independence, confronting hard consequences is the best teacher. But, when parents intervene to get their teens out of trouble, they try to repress the consequences and by doing so, an opportunity for education is lost.

Rein in Your Anger

Even as you come to know that your child has erred, it is equally important for you to control your outburst. For, listening to the child's version first and then addressing the issue with a composed mind has multiple benefits. To begin with, it calms your already ruffled youngster, besides making it easier to identify possible solutions to the problem.

When parents get angry, kids are more prone to lying. During the Class XII pre-Boards, several girls in my daughter's class flunked their papers and were asked to take a retest. Petrified of telling her parents about her poor performance, one of her friends kept agonizing over what excuse to make to go to school for the retest.

Nandini Choudhury Brahmachari narrates a bizarre incident of how overreaction by parents proves catastrophic.

> Saumya's[*] overcautious parents often scolded her whenever she was late in returning from school. Once when there was some transport problem, she persuaded her friend to come home to convince her dad and mom

that she was not loitering around. But the suspicious parents refused to listen and began scolding. Unable to face the embarrassment in front of her friend, Saumya rushed out of the house on to the terrace closely followed by her friend. Even as the friend tried to hold her back from jumping from the posh multistoreyed apartment, she plunged, taking along the hapless friend with her.

'Parents must definitely probe the reason behind violations but believe their children, at least initially,' cautions Brahmachari, who counselled the unfortunate parents. Besides, as a rule, they must never scold or admonish teenagers in front of others as it tends to have an astounding negative impact on their self-respect.

Tap the Power of Conversation

The most appropriate move for adults when faced with a predicament is to get their teenagers to talk about their troubles.

Speaking from experience, expect rejection as attempts to connect with them may be met with anger or irritation. But, no matter how much they withdraw, slam the door or roll their eyes, know that they need our love and attention. Persistence always pays and a breakthrough will come when they will let you in.

Listen to their account without judging, interrupting, criticizing or offering advice. It helps to maintain an eye contact in order to make them feel understood and valued. When you take time to listen, you get an opportunity to hear what is really going on in their minds. When they feel heard, they are more likely to be open to your thoughts or suggestions.

Before parents hasten to take charge of the situation,

they must try to encourage the children to think of possible solutions. You can narrate instances from your own knowledge and childhood. Keep in mind that the idea is to help them deal with their mistakes without telling them what to do.

It is crucial to avoid lecturing when you see they have realized their mistakes, for it is not the time to teach, but heal first. Do not be scornful or critical of teens at this weak moment. Sister Shivani of the Brahma Kumaris[17] says: 'The children need your love most when they least deserve [it].' Parents must focus on bringing kids closer even as they distance the act/wrong committed by them, emphasizes the gentle spiritual leader, who focuses on love and forgiveness as the basis of bringing about positive changes in people.

The main reason why teenagers find themselves closer to their friends is because they usually tend to be more supportive in times of stress. When parents demonstrate love and patience even when their kids err, they are sure to come closer to them.

---

[17] A worldwide spiritual movement committed to self-transformation through meditation and positive thinking.

13

Do Not Fear Their Fury

'If you cannot at first control your anger, learn to control your tongue, which like fire is a good servant, but a hard master.'

—ANONYMOUS

I once got a mail from a harried mother of two young boys. She shared her helplessness in controlling the temper tantrums of her teens, often finding herself embroiled in a shouting match with them. Incidentally, the issue of teen anger had been playing on my mind for some time. For, every time I pick up the newspaper replete with incidents of violence and aggression displayed by youngsters, I feel it is the result of inept handling of anger in the early years of their lives. Before replying to the woman, I went on to do some research on anger triggers of adolescents.

When we were children, our mother would always caution us against anger. She said it was our deadliest enemy as it blinded good sense and therefore reasoning and got us into unimaginable troubles. She implored us to conquer this enemy on our pathway to success. Mother was not wrong, but as I grew up, went to work, got married and had children of my own, I realized this so-called enemy was present just about everywhere—at school, in college, on the playgrounds, even on outings, holidays, weddings and parties. I also came to realize that no matter how much one tries, banishing anger completely from one's life appears to be a difficult proposition.

What is the way out then? Over the years, I have come to realize that it is extremely important to learn to develop the ability to decode anger and work out effective mechanisms to deal with that feeling every time it surfaces.

Decoding Anger

The first thing that we need to do is change our attitude towards anger. Often branded as regressive and unacceptable, we have always believed that anger is bad and been admonished to suppress and conquer it. But, anger is an emotion as natural and acceptable as joy or love. It is merely an appropriate response to frustration, pain, loss or neediness, point out experts. That is to say, there's nothing wrong with anger per se. It's only how one expresses the emotion that leads to all the trouble.

Neuro-linguistic Programming (NLP) expert Arpita Banerjee suggests parents, teachers and caregivers to primarily focus on decoding anger and understand the underlying reasons behind it. 'Anger is only at the surface, what you call the tip of the iceberg. We have to get to the root of the problem, understand the pattern and the anger triggers,' says the transformational coach who works with teachers, students and parents. It could be due to guilt, hurt, fear, frustration or something as basic as hunger. When we understand the source, we are automatically better equipped to handle the outbursts in a more matured manner.

As parents, we probably top the list in witnessing different expressions of anger of our children: banging of the bedroom door—the most diligently practised expression of anger by kids universally, from Patna to Pennsylvania. We can start by recognizing when our children are angry and explore the reason behind the anger—is it pain, hurt, disappointment, fear, guilt, rejection, temporary failure at something, insecurity or tension to perform? Most mothers would know even pangs of hunger cause children to fly off their handles unnecessarily. Once we have identified the reason behind their fury, only then can we help them find healthy ways to release their steam.

Pays to Be Patient

An important thing to remember is not to lose your own cool (at least at that point of time!) when kids appear to be in the throes of rage. Because two angry people—parent and child—can only put the house on fire or spell disaster.

No matter how much adolescents try to act like adults, we need to keep in mind they do not have a fully-developed brain. Therefore, they indulge in all kinds of impulsive and inappropriate behaviour like yelling and screaming. But when we scream back at our children, it only ends up escalating the argument as both of us are then acting on the same level. Not only that, it keeps the fight going that much longer. Moreover, when we yell back at our child, it amounts to giving the remote control of our temper in their hands. By bringing us down to his level, the child feels empowered because he can make us lose control by getting us angry any time he wants. On the other hand, it is certainly not a good idea to hit children because it only shows them that the way to gain control of a situation is to use physical force. Besides, you run the risk of only worsening the entire situation.

Role modelling is one of the key components of teaching kids how to behave. Says behavioural therapist James Lehman: 'You've got to model the behaviour you want to see from your child.' If you do not want your kid to yell at you, do not yell at him. If you do not want your child to curse, do not curse.

Train to be Anger Smart

It may sound preposterous to some, but we need to tell our children it's alright to be angry, at times. But, what is not all right is expressing it in a way that hurts us or others. Just like we exhort our kids to be street-smart in order to survive in this world, we also need to emphasize on becoming 'anger smart'. This includes identifying anger triggers and chalking out strategies on how to react to anger. Arpita Banerjee recommends what she keenly practices with her clients as well as her two young boys—the Observe, Analyse, Control and Change (OACC) technique. It includes observing the cause of anger, analysing the pattern and controlling the outbursts to bring about a change in situation.

Some Handy Tips to Handle Anger

- Drinking a glass of cool water when you feel the heady rush of fury is like virtually splashing water over fire.
- Make a concerted decision not to use harsh language or physical violence, no matter what the provocation may be.
- Chewing the food well before swallowing reduces instances of anger outbursts, point out both doctors and spiritual leaders.
- A healthy body and an active mind engaged in productive work also ensure one will not get angry easily.
- Counsellors suggest physical and creative activities like

sports, music and painting help ease a restless mind.
- Having a cooling-off ritual like taking a walk, listening to music, star gazing or watching the fishes in an aquarium often prove very effective.

In his path-breaking book on self-improvement, *Change Your Thoughts, Change Your Life*, Dr Wayne Dyer says you should vow never to start a fight. Stay on the defensive side of disputes, 'play the guest' rather than making the first move. Remind yourself that when you start a fight, you'd be battling with yourself, he advises. The tip works well for both parents as well as children.

Concurrently, children should be taught to forgive and forget early on in life so that they do not hold grudges for long whether against peers or adults. It is often these pent-up feelings of hurt and humiliation which transform into hatred and aggression in youngsters. So, handling anger is crucial as expressing it through explosive behaviour or keeping it bottled up since childhood can have serious repercussions. According to experts like Ghosal and Prakash, Silent Anger is what leads to passive aggressive behaviour (PAB) which can prove dangerous and self-destructive for children. There are two kinds of children—the ones who react, say, when scolded and others who may not react instantly, but after a while do something to hurt the 'perpetrator' or themselves. This is passive aggressive behaviour which we need to watch out for.

Instead of allowing anger to get out of control, we need to help our children become more self-aware and know their feelings. I sincerely believe when parents, caregivers and teachers help children figure out how to cope with anger, they can reduce incidence of road rage, domestic violence and the overall aggression displayed by youths.

Tap Its Productiveness

A couple of years ago, our daughter Anukriti, refused to heed all requests by her vocal music teacher to do riyaaz (practice). As a result, she did not prepare well even a week before her annual Hindustani Classical Music exams. Finding her far from satisfactory to face an examiner, her otherwise friendly teacher curtly asked her to quit the exams, instead of making a fool of him as well as herself. Anukriti was hurt and angry beyond words. Both of us (her father and I) saw her seething with rage, but preferred to leave her alone to brood over what she considered an insult by her teacher.

The next morning, we woke up to the sound of the harmonium, followed by her vocals. That week she practised her ragas like a girl possessed. Needless to say, on the final day, she surprised her teacher with her near perfect rendition of her choice raga.

Since then, it has become a thing between us to keep going back to that day to remember how we have the power to direct our anger to achieve whatever we strive for. So it suffices to say, this emotion called anger/fury/rage, which is more often than not tagged with negativity, can actually be tapped for its productivity. One can effectively channelize it to act as a source of strength to bring about positive changes. Moreover, when we redirect anger at injustice and other wrongs perpetrated on the society, we unwittingly indulge in self-enhancing activities.

One can recall it was the anger of M.K. Gandhi, a 22-year-old barrister at the gross injustice of being thrown out of a train's first-class compartment in South Africa despite having a valid ticket, that not just altered his life, but the course of humanity. From a simple Indian notary travelling in a foreign land, Gandhi gradually transformed into the fearless Mahatma with an indefatigable spirit.[18]

All said and done, if you feel your teen is unable to get a hold on his/her aggression, do not hesitate to seek professional help. For all you know, it can help save not one, but several lives.

---

[18]See Raksha Bharadia, *Roots and Wings*.

14
Calling Out the Demon Called Exam Stress

'What is defeat? Nothing but education...'

—WENDELL PHILLIPS

Examinations are what I call the 'watershed' or the defining moment of our parenting. It's that time when most parents make an all-out bid to provide every possible input to help their children perform better. While some stay up late in the night studying or making notes to aid their efforts, others pamper their taste buds with the best culinary delights so that kids bring forth their best on the answer sheets. There are many who also invoke the gods and goddesses to stand behind their wards showering them with intellect and wisdom.

Even as we strive to calm their frayed nerves, we have to simultaneously work hard to get a hold on our own wits. For, examinations mean upheavals in most households in terms of lost notebooks, alternate loss of appetite or monstrous cravings for munchies, erratic sleep syndromes and examination eve pangs. All this clearly requires parents to summon all their expertise and patience for surviving it all.

Then there is that realization only on the eve of their exams that one should have put in more through the year. It calls for every bit of restraint on the part of parents who may be tempted to give kids a sound tongue-lashing of 'I told you so...' for that would hardly salvage the present situation.

Whatever said and done, exams can be stressful times for children, parents as well as teachers. But as prudent, hands-on parents, we have the ability to help children dominate this so-called 'devil'.

Differentiate Between Stress and Pressure

To begin with, we need to understand the difference between the terms 'stress' and 'pressure'. They are often used interchangeably, but, in fact, are quite different. Pressure can be positive and useful to complete deadlines, but when prolonged, it can become negative. Depending on how a person perceives and reacts to it, pressure can lead to stress.

Pressure to perform well during exams is natural. In fact, it goads us to work harder, think faster and more effectively and can help us improve performance.

Every student knows he/she has to appear for exams at certain times of the year. Yet very few are focused on preparing themselves to face them. Children who study regularly throughout the year, experience only a mild pressure to simply revise their work before examinations. On the other hand, those who postpone studies till the last minute find themselves in a quandary. They spend sleepless nights cramming the lessons. The syllabus seems huge and teachers deficient. Their notes are inadequate and the world appears unfair. Needless to say, all this causes immense stress and tension which often gets transmitted to the entire household of the examinee.

Symptoms of Fear

Once when we were driving our teen to her examination centre for her first Board exam, a car menacingly overtook ours from the left. A nervous student poring over her books on the rear seat made clear to us the urgency of the driver. We had hardly proceeded a hundred yards when the same car screeched to a halt and the anxious girl jumped out throwing up uncontrollably on the roadside. The parents accompanying her clearly looked helpless.

Come examination time and even the bravehearts are seized by fear and anxiety pertaining to performance. But when the anxiety levels become overwhelming, causing insomnia, loss of appetite or depression, it tends to threaten their peace as well as performance. According to a medical expert, Dr Madhukar Prakash, central council member, Indian Medical Association, when someone is under great stress, the brain begins to send alarm signals causing the release of excessive amounts of adrenalin into the body. This can lead to different physical, mental and emotional manifestations of fear.

The physical symptoms could range from possible skin breakouts, teeth grinding, nail biting and fidgeting to shortness of breath, nausea, dysentery and stomach cramps. The mental symptoms could include insomnia, loss of memory or going blank during the exam. On the emotional side, people can get cranky and irritable, indulging in yelling and crying or getting sad and depressed.[19]

Convert Tension into Energy

Tension during exams is normal. Sometimes, a lot of it is passed

---

[19]'Exam Phobia—Cause and Remedies', https://targetstudy.com/articles/exam-phobia-cause-and-remedies.html

on to them by the family or even the school in a bid to get them to work harder. But it is important to know we can convert this tension into tremendous energy. Athletes and sportsmen compulsorily suffer from nervous tension before every event, points out Cedric M. Kenny, but it only tones their muscles and puts them on razor-sharp alert mode.

The best way to help children overcome psychosomatic breakdowns is to make them learn lessons from their sports icons. Kenny exhorts students to use tension to their advantage by converting it into an energy force. So, during exam time, parents need to feed the subconscious minds of the children with positive inputs of determination, conviction and confidence.

Resort to Frequent Pep Talks

Quite a few parents believe that the best way to get their wards cracking before exams is by dangling a carrot for good performance. For instance, 'If you score above 90 per cent in your Boards, we will buy you an iPhone'. They believe promising material goods is the best form of motivation for this generation. And then we crib our youngsters only swear by their material acquisitions!

The best way to motivate children to work hard and transform their stress into constructive energy is by having frequent encouraging conversations. These pep talks should be aimed at highlighting their strengths, reminding them to be positive, believing in themselves and leaving the rest to God. Creating your own mantra for success for your child is another good idea to help combat exam stress. Like, 'Do your best and leave the rest'.

Distractions Galore

Inadequate and poor preparations for exams are often the outcome of countless distractions that children cope with today. Internet, television, smartphones, gaming, music, mall hopping and parties—all these demons of distraction (read entertainment) are a bane of modern life. Unfortunately, they seem to be multiplying by the dozen, consuming their time, attention and commitment. These diversions drive down productivity, affect concentration and come in the way of their academic goals. Every second parent I come across appears to be grappling with the impact of these distractions which are at its peak in the teenage years. Ironically, these are also the years which require consistent efforts in academics as children take their crucial exams.

The benefits notwithstanding, the Internet is by far one of the biggest distractions for our children. Almost every book, music album and video is just a click away. Even the most conscientious kids concede that amidst working on assignments they often find themselves checking out YouTube videos.

Smartphones, with their ever-increasing set of features, only seem to compound the predicament for our children. Watching the speed and deftness of their fingers on WhatsApp and Facebook Messenger or while playing Temple Run and Candy Crush can be rather awe-inspiring. But, parents would rather have kids display similar skills in writing out their answer sheets too!

I remember being overjoyed when Anukriti handed me her phone asking me to put it away until her Board exams. But, the delight dwindled when I found her studying with her headphones on—listening to music. I realized sourly that you cannot deprive children of every gadget. About 80 per cent of teens listen to music while studying, claiming it keeps their mind active.

The innumerable get-togethers—from birthdays and batch parties to school farewells—that the youngsters attend act as another major diversion.

I sometimes feel truly sorry for our children who have to manoeuvre their way through a maze of diversions to reach their goals. As parents, don't you think we lived a far easier life with just the television and the radio to give us our dose of entertainment?

Work Out Solutions

Coming to possible solutions, I think we need to strike a bargain with our children. For, anything imposed from the top is bound to be grossly violated.

- It's a good idea to fix time for Internet browsing, watching YouTube videos or the television so that kids do not fuss when you switch off the Wi-Fi during the study hours.
- If they insist on listening to music while studying, ensure it is only instrumental music as one with lyrics clearly engages the mind.
- Get them to choose, say a couple of parties (as a blanket ban on outings can spell trouble for their social life!) But, that too, they can attend only after completing a certain portion of their syllabus.
- One must convince the children to give up their cell

phones at least temporarily during or before exams. If not, then ensure their phones are on silent mode and away from reach while studying so they do not keep checking messages. What we need to emphasize is multitasking while studying is clearly no good.

Cool Head, A Must

It is imperative to insist on a good night's sleep of at least seven hours before an exam as pulling an all-nighter spells disaster. Proper rest of the mind and body helps rejuvenate an overworked brain, enabling better recollection of the revised matter.

Keeping the body refuelled with healthy nutritious food is equally important during exam preparations. Eating before and during exam time can keep anxieties and tensions at bay and improve memory. Practising relaxation techniques like breathing exercises or yoga, taking adequate breaks for walks to get fresh air, listening to music or laughing with friends and family in order to de-stress are also essential.

While the course of one's career to a great extent does depend on the Boards or competitive exams, excessive harping on the fact by the parents can only become counterproductive. Desist from talking about results like 'what if you don't get a certain percentage…' or discussing the high cut-offs required for college admissions, once the exams have begun.

What some of us don't realize is too much pressure to perform can cause teens to fall off the edge. And certainly, nothing is more vital than the health and well-being of our children.

15
Enters the Dragon—Social Media

'Teens turn to, and are obsessed with whichever environment allows them to connect to friends.'

—DANAH BOYD

Several years ago when we were travelling to Singapore, I was blown away by practically everything—spotlessly clean surroundings, child-friendly amenities, organized traffic and zero honk roads. But, something that particularly caught my attention was the complete silence in the MRT (Mass Rapid Transit system, akin to our Metro rail) trains. I noticed that practically everyone (standing or sitting) was engaged on their cell phones. With their rapidly changing expressions, I could make out they were either chatting or watching videos, totally oblivious to the world around.

Not long after our visit, social media—which till then was a dormant dragon (with only Facebook and MSN Messenger being in use)—reared its head in India too. People—young and old—began to be sucked into this whirlwind with all its ills and thrills. Today, social media is like a full-grown dragon which guzzles down everything that comes its way—our time, attention and money. The worst victims are clearly the youngsters whose immature brains are unable to recognize and ward off addiction to social media.

Meanwhile, social networking sites have multiplied by the dozen. Interestingly, Facebook is passé, considered for the 'oldies' now. More popular among the youngsters now are Instagram, Snapchat, Twitter, Tumblr, Pinterest (for its DIY stuff) and YouTube (for the visual content). As a result, the lives of most teenagers revolve around hits and clicks. Parents are either left fuming at their preoccupation or resign to what they call 'a changed thought process of this generation'. But the fact remains: Excessive use of social media, which was designed to provide simple means of communication with friends, has led to a trail of social, mental and physical problems for the child.

Research shows most teens are extremely deficient in face-to-face communication skills even as they are adept at online communication. According to the Pew Research Center, one in three teens sends over 100 text messages a day. More than half of teens use texting to communicate daily with friends, versus only 33 per cent who regularly talk face-to-face.[20] They also majorly miss out on personal growth and development, academic discipline and learning. On the mental front, excessive dependence on social media can lead to anxiety, depression, erosion of confidence and even suicidal tendencies. Impact of this addiction on teens' health is equally alarming as it can cause insomnia, eating disorders in terms of binge eating or anorexia.

Signs of Addiction

While counsellors across the world would agree social media is a necessary evil of this generation, parents and guardians can certainly be proactive in controlling their obsession.

---

[20]Laurie Hollman, 'What's Happened to Face-to-Face Conversation With Teens? Cell Phone "Addictions",' HuffPost, 6 October 2015, https://www.huffingtonpost.com/laurie-hollman-phd/whats-happened-to-facetof_b_8209706.html

Recognize signs of fixation in teens or tweens when:

- They are unable to refrain from checking their updates: It is common to catch youngsters constantly plugged in to their smartphones, perpetually engaged in online activity.
- They show anxiety in absence of Internet connectivity: They feel restless and insecure if deprived of Internet connection.
- Their sleeping pattern is changed: Children who spend excessive time on the Internet, invariably tend to stay up till late in the night, dozing off only at dawn.

Its Impact

As parents, we often notice that kids instantly adopt what is popular among their friends. If, for instance, your daughter's friends use Instagram, the photo-sharing app invariably becomes her favourite simply out of a 'fear of missing out' (FOMO) on the in-thing. The teen will scrupulously follow the same celebrities and upload similar stories as her friends so she can stay up to date and participate in discussions when they meet. This also explains the strange phenomenon—if one person decides to share the picture and details of his meal or an outing, everyone else tends to do the same.

According to psychologists, constant social media activity wherein people spend hours updating new statuses, uploading pictures, commenting on walls, playing games, reading other people's updates and searching for new friends to add, fosters a stimulus-reward mechanism. Whenever teens and tweens (even adults who are engrossed in online activity) post something on a social media site and get a flurry of 'likes' from friends and followers, it brings about an immediate positive feedback.

However, being caught in a web of constant online activity can be emotionally draining as the body begins spewing stress hormones. School performance begins to suffer and children experience mood swings that go beyond typical teen moodiness.

Real-time Interaction Pangs

Modern teens happen to conduct most of their communication while looking at a screen, missing out on very critical social skills—the ability to read and understand people's body language and facial expressions.

It is easier to keep your guard up when you're texting as there's little at stake. You are not hearing or watching the effect your words have on the other person. That's why, children find a telephonic conversation far 'too intense' and prefer interacting on, say, WhatsApp.

Recent studies show socially insecure and anxious people are more likely to get addicted to social networking sites as they find it easier to communicate via social media.

Erosion of Family Time

An ironical WhatsApp forward shows a modern family sitting at the dining table where all are stealthily busy on their handsets. As ludicrous as it may seem, social media has the potential to make people, particularly children, drift away from spending quality time with family. This can certainly erode the bonding between parents and children. 'Internet and social media addiction has definitely cut into the roots of family,' concedes Dr Latika Prakash. While television had created latent consumers in children, social media has only turned them into aggressive, voracious consumers as practically everything they see on screens and glitzy showrooms can be theirs on the click of a mouse. Unfortunately, it's the youngsters who are bitten hardest by this terrible bug of 'more is still less' as their anxiety to look chic, cool and happening is highest.

Meanwhile, most parents of young children complain they hardly have proper conversations with them. Some of my friends, whose kids have gone away for higher studies, complain that even when they come home for vacations, they remain glued to their smartphones or laptops and hardly interact.

Obsessing Over Selfies

In the last few years, youngsters seem to have been gripped by the appalling 'selfie mania'. One can spot them practically everywhere striking ludicrous poses with faces contorted like ducks and uploading the perfect selfie to social networking sites.

At a Parent-Teacher Meet, I once overheard a hassled mother crib: 'I think my girl is toiling for her exams, but on checking I find her taking selfies with her books.' The teacher instantly started lecturing the girl on how she should take her studies more seriously. I noticed that while the teen nodded vigorously, she wore a distant look in her eyes, probably wondering how a selfie would look now—captioned 'Being fired by the teacher!'

Incidentally, it's common for teens to participate in activities with a focus on how it can 'appear' in the social media realm. So, appearing to have fun becomes more important than actually enjoying the moment. Seeking people's approval and attention and basing your self-esteem on the number of 'likes' you garner is a niggling fallout of the selfie mania.

According to Ranjana Roy, a senior counsellor with a reputed Kolkata school, admiring themselves and seeking to know what others feel about them is part of growing up for adolescents. 'Nevertheless, too much dependence on public approval spells trouble,' she concedes.

Clicking selfies and uploading them is not inappropriate per se, but how much should be no more is what is pertinent.[21]

Body Shaming

Body shaming or putting down another person due to an individual physical trait is another deplorable activity on social media. By uploading provocative pictures, youngsters, particularly girls, often find themselves engaged in a reckless race of who looks better than whom. Body shaming among teens is a disturbing reality which at times can assume catastrophic proportions—as in the case of a teen from a small town in West Bengal (mentioned earlier in the chapter titled 'Accept Peers are Vital').

Experts like Brahmachari point out that the vulnerability of teens is intensified by the fact that with social media, approval of friends becomes most important, eclipsing the value of parental approval.

The other big danger that comes from communicating

---

[21]'Parenteen: Beat That Selfie mania', 1 August 2015. Source: The Times of India Group. © BCCL. All Rights Reserved

on social media is that it has become easier to be cruel. The sort of things that people text on these social sites, one would never imagine saying it to someone's face. Moreover, such online criticism could be far more damaging, as you may visit it again and again unless you delete it; plus it is likely to spread rapidly among the teens' friend circle on social media sites. Unfortunately, not just youngsters, but even quite a few adults indulge in this form of nastiness online.

Creation of Lusty Consumers

Among other things, the Internet has enabled just about everyone to peek into the closets of the rich and the famous. No wonder, Bollywood style icons are passé as our youngsters now look up to Hollywood, London, Milan, among other places, to emulate their fashion statements. That's not all, besides whetting the appetites of a generation of people, the Internet has moved on to helping them actualize their dreams of possessing glamorous outfits and accessories by the click of a mouse. That is to say, social media is creating an ever-increasing breed of lusty consumers out of youngsters who will not stop short of acquiring the outfits or products they are exposed to. But, no matter how much of clothes, accessories or gadgets one buys, it always falls short of their requirement. It may be true with some adults too, but teens are bitten hardest by this terrible bug of 'more is still less' as their anxiety to look cool, chic and happening is the highest.

As the children fall prey to aggressive marketing and elusive fashion statements, parents are left with a pile of clothing which gets outdated faster than their parents' dwindling bank balance!

Focus on Solutions

Unfortunately, there are only limited solutions to weaning our children from the obsessions of the Internet. Restrictive solutions can often be counterproductive as the Internet is, after all, the fundamental language, a world force that one can hardly survive without. We can only practise directional parenting, becoming proactive in following their online interests and attention.

- Work out clear, solid rules for your child's technology use in order to ensure a productive, well-rounded teen.
- Provide some reasonable limitations on their social media time to ensure they remain active in the real world too. Get them to set a timer for their online activity, exhorting them to test their own will power.
- Get them to turn off notifications which only act as reminders that something is always happening in the online world.
- Engage in constructive activities like painting, craft making, theatre or sports which require substantial self-discipline. The more involved they are in sports and other activities, the less time they'll spend on their devices.

A child who is active, engaged and social will naturally spend far less time on social media and more time in the 'real' world.

16

Emphasize on Safety Before Fun

> *'The journey in between what you once were
> and who you are now becoming is where the
> dance of life really takes place.'*
>
> —BARBARA De ANGELIS

One's days of youth are often synonymous with high spirits and gaiety. Every youngster desires to make the most of his youthfulness, indulging in every fun activity he/she can manage. Sometimes, in the course of having uninhibited fun and merriment, with no adult supervision, children end up making bad choices for themselves. This is when they unconsciously tend to compromise on their safety. And lo! In no time, all the fun and enjoyment can turn into danger and disaster.

Shoojit Sircar's *Pink* touched the chords of young and old alike with its terse plot, unravelling the aftermath of an outing of youngsters that goes terribly wrong. The thought-provoking film brings to the fore how a woman's perception, and therefore, approach towards experiencing freedom—in terms of having a fun evening in male company and drinks—should not be misconstrued as an affirmation of the male's desire to be physically close to her. However, watching the film as a parent of a young girl, I also painfully realized how unmindful action, flippant behaviour in public and small errors in judgement by youngsters can have a crucial bearing on their safety and security.

In the course of his dialogues in the movie, master thespian Amitabh Bachchan scorns the typical Indian mentality to judge a girl's character by the length of her skirt, the time she comes home or the male companions she has. The dialogues, besides being a rap on our society, also serve as a reality check for youngsters in general and girls in particular. For they need to live their lives in complete awareness of the nature of society we live in.

Anukriti, who had volunteered to accompany us for the movie, walked out of the theatre rather pensively. 'Gosh, it's a scary world out there, mom! I don't think I want to go anywhere away from your cocoon, not even for my higher studies,' she said wistfully. I hastened to assuage the fears of my girl even as we discussed ways of preserving one's dignity, self-respect and security in variable conditions.

As we bring up our girls to be strong, smartly independent and believe in themselves, we also need to apprise them of the kind of society we operate in, the mindsets they will encounter in it and the dangers they are most likely to face.

As for the boys, they too need a firm grounding on how to conduct themselves with female friends, respect their privacy and personal spaces. And most importantly, accept their 'no' without taking it as an affront to their masculinity.[22]

Reason Behind Recklessness

According to experts, children's appetite for thrill and excitement can be explained by two physical phenomena taking place in their bodies. To begin with, it is important to remember that the brain grows from back to front. So, while the part which seeks excitement and gratification, develops early, the frontal lobe—the

---

[22]Parenteen: Bring Out the Power of Pink', 3 October 2016. Source: The Times of India Group. © BCCL. All Rights Reserved

seat of decision-making or the part which makes them responsible for their actions—is the last to develop. Add to this the hormonal assault (excess flow of testosterone and oestrogen) triggered by puberty. The result is a heady cocktail of impulsive behaviour and sensation-seeking thrill, so often visible in the teens.

That is the reason why youngsters are so prone to skirting with danger, driving recklessly or challenging rules, says Cedric M. Kenny.

Courting Danger is (Not) Fun

- Pune was rocked by the death of fourteen college students who drowned on a college picnic in Alibaug. The youngsters, all aged between 18 to 23 years, were forewarned by the locals about the treacherous waters. Refusing to heed, the group ventured into the waters and got swept away by the tide. (1 February 2016)[23]
- Two teenagers from a south Kolkata college, who went for a joyride to Mandarmani (a beach town in West Bengal) with two others after lying to their parents that they were spending Saturday night at a friend's place, drowned in the sea during the morning high tide. (29 May 2017)[24]

---

[23] Vijay Singh and Umesh K. Parida, 'Tragedy at Murud Beach: 14 Pune students on a picnic drown in sea', TNN, 1 February 2016, https://timesofindia.indiatimes.com/india/Tragedy-at-Murud-beach-14-Pune-students-on-a-picnic-drown-in-sea/articleshow/50807743.cms

[24] 'Fun turns to tragedy: 2 teenagers drown at Mandarmoni', *The Asian Age*, 29 May 2017, http://www.asianage.com/metros/kolkata/290517/fun-turns-

- A 19-year-old engineering student of IIT-Mandi drowned in the Uhal River apparently while taking a selfie. (17 February 2017)[25]
- Four college students on a joyride died in a fatal car crash in Ludhiana. Ironically, the youngsters had posted their last video on a social networking site a few minutes before the accident, wherein they were all enjoying music and singing inside the car. The Honda City was allegedly being driven at a speed of 150 kmph before it hit a curbstone. (7 January 2017)[26]

The list of joyrides and fun moments gone terribly wrong is endless. Youngsters often perceive alerts and warnings pertaining to speeding, smoking, swimming or straying into dangerous waters with considerable disdain. The consequences of such an attitude are, more often than not, fatal. The ruin is, however, not only the keepsake of the life snuffed, but also belongs to the others who are left behind.

The fact is children are vulnerable everywhere and as parents it is natural to worry about their safety. But good parenting requires developing healthy ways to help them stay out of trouble.

---

to-tragedy-2-teenagers-drown-at-mandarmoni.html

[25]'IIT Mandi student drowns allegedly while clicking selfie in Uhal river', *The Tribune*, 17 February 2017, http://www.tribuneindia.com/news/himachal/community/iit-mandi-student-drowns-allegedly-while-clicking-selfie-in-uhal-river/365494.html

[26]'Four youths killed in mishap near Ludhiana', *The Tribune*, 7 January 2017, http://www.tribuneindia.com/news/punjab/community/four-youths-killed-in-mishap-near-ludhiana/346950.html

While we must evolve our own customized rules regarding strangers, animals, home and school safety for our young children, it is equally important to make our older children also follow meticulous safety measures while on the road, near the waters, at parties or whenever out with friends.

Safety on Roads

According to statistics, more youths (between 15 to 29 years of age) die due to road crashes than due to any illness or homicide. That is to say, road crashes are a serious threat to youths everywhere. Some of the factors responsible for crashes include driving without helmets or seat belts, over speeding and drunk- or distracted-driving (busy on their cell phones). Speeding of vehicles to get that momentary adrenalin rush, concede police, is a major killer. The Kolkata police, for instance, have been struggling to rein in a perilous practice of young bikers indulging in high-speed racing down flyovers and deserted roads after midnight.

'Juvenile justice law looks at teenagers as victims and not criminals,' points out Superintendent of Railway Police, Sealdah, Sabyasachi. Since the law is tilted in their favour, there is often very little fear among them. This is where proactive parenting is required to rein in unruly youngsters before tragedy strikes.

- It is insensible to indulge our children and allow them to drive four-wheelers until they are 18 years of age. Parents who hand over car keys to kids, endanger not just their lives but also those of several others on the roads.

- If you must get your child a bike to ensure easy conveyance, it is advisable to get speed limit devices installed which arrest the top speed of the vehicles.
- Insist, pull up and punish youngsters yourselves if you find them under the influence of alcohol. Remember every act of indulgence brazens them up to commit the next mistake.

Security Parameters for Partying

Most tweens and teens like to party which includes attending concerts or college festivals and having get togethers at home or outside. Whether you like it or not, you cannot hold them back for long as chances are they will begin to lie and go out, anyway. So, it's always better to agree upon certain guidelines with your child. When they do go out, following a few simple steps can go a long way in ensuring their safety even as they let their hair down and enjoy freely.

- It is scrupulous to prevail upon our youngsters to share important details about their outings. Be fully informed about who is throwing the party, who their companions are and their expected time of return. Insist on taking the host's phone number. Avoid going to sleep without letting them back in for there are innumerable instances when long drives after parties result in accidents or run-ins with the law.
- Even as we insist they take only soft drinks and not alcohol, it is important to remind them never to leave their food or drink unattended. Children should be

aware that drugs used for sexual assault are often slipped into drinks.
- Advise them to stay in well-lit places and stick to the group. Categorically tell them to avoid going out with a person they've just met at the party. They must know, not all dangerous strangers are rude or domineering right away.
- Being street-smart is equally important. Children need to be aware of strangers, both men and women, who make easy conversation and get important information about people without them even realizing it. Remember, if a stranger tells you where he or she lives, it doesn't mean you too have to tell him/her where you live.
- Advise your kids not to talk about sex with strangers. I have noticed how sex jokes are often used by devious men as icebreakers with females in a group. Youngsters (girls in particular) need to be cautious when communicating with people they don't know, especially if the conversation starts to assume sexual connotations or physical details. By any chance, do not lead them on—you don't want to be the target of a predator's grooming.
- Tell them to be equally smart when using a cell phone. It is sensible to be wary of who they share their number with.
- Avoid getting into arguments with strangers as you never know their temperament. A fun evening can easily transform into something nasty and aggressive.
- Never get into a car with a driver who has been drinking.

- Always follow your gut feeling. Leave the party if you do not feel safe and comfortable. Call up parents, elder siblings or cousins to pick you up immediately.

Customize Your Safety Strategy

Parents can evolve individual strategies and safety measures for their children like using code words (pre-decided by the family) on the phone. If kids are in trouble, saying the code word will indicate they are unable to talk openly and need to be picked up right away.

It is advisable to have 'safety-check conversations' with youngsters every now and then. For, I believe it's all right to be paranoid about their safety than be sorry for life.

Nevertheless, one need not scare the wits out of the children every time they step out. It is important to inculcate in them the habit of taking some responsibility for their own safety. Educate them to trust their instincts and be aware of what is going on around them, instead of being engrossed in their gadgets. They need to remember focussing on safety will not hamper their fun. On the contrary, it will only make sure they can continue having it.

17
It's Time to Tackle Underage Drinking

'The task ahead of us is never as great as the power behind us.'

—ALCOHOLICS ANONYMOUS

A friend was aghast when her 15-year-old daughter returned from an after-exam party and confessed she had alcohol mixed with Cola. Shocked that the youngsters had free-flowing alcohol to celebrate the end of their pre-Boards, my friend called me up to share her agony. I strived to pacify the concerns of a fearful mother for her otherwise sober and sensible girl. The silver lining, I pointed out, was at least the child realized what she did was wrong and had the honesty to confide in her mother.

That afternoon, as I sat down to research the topic of underage drinking, I came by a disturbing piece of information—alcohol is indeed the drug of choice among children and young adults across the globe.

Disturbing Statistics

According to a report by the World Health Organization (WHO) and the National Institute on Alcohol Abuse and Alcoholism (NIAAA), the number of Indian teens consuming alcohol is increasing alarmingly. 'Harmful drinking is on the rise among young people and women in many OECD (Organisation for Economic Cooperation and Development) countries, partly due to alcohol becoming more available, more affordable and more effectively advertised,' said a 2015 report by the OECD. By harmful drinking they mean consuming too much alcohol too quickly, which seriously damages a person's health besides putting other people's lives at risk. The report percentage of under-15 boys who have not had alcohol has gone down from 44 per cent to 30 per cent and for girls it has decreased from 50 per cent to 31 per cent, reveals another study done by the OECD whereas that of girls decreased from 50 per cent to 31 per cent.[27]

As per recent studies conducted by an NGO called Community against Drunken Driving, of the 1,000 youngsters who go to pubs and bars, nearly 62 per cent are in the age group of 14–21 years even though the minimum legal drinking age group across major cities varies between 21 and 25 years. In big cities like Delhi and Mumbai, youngsters start drinking as early as 14 years of age when they are only in middle school. One often comes across bizarre instances of students bringing vodka or gin in their water bottles to school and sharing swigs with friends even during their classes.

Alcohol, it may be pointed out, is a brain depressant and gets absorbed quickly in the blood stream from the stomach and the small intestine. It contains ethanol, an intoxicating agent, which produces mind-altering effects and even a small quantity can impair judgement required to take crucial decisions. That definitely explains the high instances of road accidents caused by inebriated youngsters or even adults.

---

[27]OECD, 'OECD outlines action for governments to tackle heavy cost of harmful drinking', 5 December 2015, http://www.oecd.org/health/oecdoutlinesactionforgovernmentstotackleheavycostofharmfuldrinking.htm

Reasons Behind the Rise

Look around and one can notice there has been a considerable decline in taboos against alcohol consumption in the Indian society. Today, social drinking—both by men as well as women—is increasingly being accepted. Naturally, the youngsters are also finding it easier to access, taste and enjoy a tipple every now and then.

'Parents in India have suddenly become too liberal and seldom say a firm "no" to kids,' rues a school principal. Most parents allow young children to have a Breezer which they feel contains only 4 per cent alcohol. Within no time, these children graduate to having hard drinks like whisky or vodka, she adds. Meanwhile, according to counsellors, lack of parental oversight, peer pressure and easy availability of disposable money in their hands are contributing to the sudden rise in the consumption of alcohol freely by the youngsters.

Temptations Abound

Add to that the travails of puberty and the need to assert independence among adolescents. Seeking thrills often leads to experimenting with alcohol. On the other hand, the curiosity to try out the forbidden spurs the temptation to taste liquor. 'Just try it at least once' is how it starts, confess some youngsters rather candidly.

There is also this strong desire among children to 'fit in' as the hip and happening always associate celebration and fun with alcohol. 'Most of my friends I hung out with used to drink and I found it rather cool,' shrugs 15-year-old Anahita*. 'So, it was natural for me to join them. It wasn't really forced on me,' she adds in the same breath.

Surprisingly, acquiring these drinks is hardly an issue as the teens claim to either source them from their parents' collection or buy them from the supermarkets or stores.

Aggressive Advertising

Advertising majors today hire shrewd psychologists who understand teen obsession with being cool. Clearly targeting the youth in the language they understand, these companies are trying to hard sell their products by projecting a certain image of being 'cool, hip and successful'. Constant exposure to commercials, which promise popularity, fun and rocking relationships, is consequently turning youngsters into insatiable consumers.

Persistent promotion of beer or alcohol on social media through surrogate advertising (as direct advertisement of tobacco and alcoholic beverages is banned in India) only adds fuel to fire. When teens watch commercials in which men and women are having a splendid time with a suggested toast in hand, the subtle encouragement to drink and have fun only gets imprinted on their impressionable minds.[28]

A worrisome finding by a series of research across the world reveals that irrespective of what parents might do to shield their kids from liquor advertising, alcohol marketers are doing their best to reach them any which way. Studies prove that the more young people are exposed to alcohol advertising,

---

[28]'Parenteen: Address underage drinking now', 28 January 2016. Source: The Times of India Group. © BCCL. All Rights Reserved

the more likely it is that they are going to drink or indulge in binge drinking. When teens drink, they tend to do it intensively, often consuming four to five drinks at a time. Binge drinking is a pattern of consuming alcohol that brings blood alcohol concentration (BAC) to 0.08 grams per cent. This translates to consuming over five drinks (men) and four or more drinks (women) in about two hours.

Grim Consequences

The consequences, more often than not, are disastrous.

- Drinking at a young age greatly increases the risk of developing alcohol problems later in life. Psychologists point out that the younger the adolescents are when they start drinking, the more likely they are to engage in risky behaviours like using drugs, having unprotected sex at an early age or performing poorly in academics.
- Moreover, as youngsters have one too many, they often end up puking, fainting or losing control of their emotions. Unable to get a hold on themselves, they tend to indulge in disorderly conduct in public.
- Teens, who are sloshed, can end up endangering not just their own lives, but also of those around them. Binge drinking is roughly estimated to cause nearly 5,000 deaths of people within 12 to 21 years of age every year. Speeding, rash driving or tendency to overestimate their driving skills—all contribute to the high crash rate among young drivers.
- Apart from accidents, point out police, the youth's affinity for alcohol is also responsible for increasing

homicides, rapes and suicides.
- Doctors contend having alcohol during puberty can upset the critical hormonal balance necessary for normal development of organs, muscles and bones.
- Some researchers believe heavy drinking at an age when the brain is still developing may cause lasting impairments in its functions, including memory, coordination and motor skills.

Resort to Early Solutions

As parents and guardians, we must equip ourselves with knowledge and tactfulness to handle difficult situations in the lives of our children. That is to say, we must intervene in a timely manner to bring about a change in their attitude and intention so they are able to resist the 'pro-drinking' influences and opportunities which tend to surround them.

Tackle it Head-on

Discussing with them the dangers and risks associated with drinking is essentially the first step. While most parents recognize the importance of discussing alcohol with kids, they are not always sure when to initiate this talk. It is crucial to know adolescents are often nervous and confused when faced with their first opportunity to try alcohol. Initiate open discussions on the topic early on, instead of waiting till you catch them drinking.

Outsmart Advertisers

We need to use the alarming findings about advertisers particularly targeting youngsters as a wake-up call for parents. You can call it waging our very own war against furtive advertisers who are out to get our children. Parents must make a concerted effort to discourage children from mindlessly buying into the advertisers' gimmicks and therefore validate their products. Sit with them and help them analyse commercials, prodding them to rethink what's cool, instead of what the marketers want them to think. This way, you can possibly arrest the negative trend so vigorously encouraged by alcoholic beverage manufacturers.

Mark Out Clear Rules

It is advisable to communicate your values and set definite rules against drinking. Youngsters are less likely to drink when they know that parents and other important adults in their lives have strong feelings about it. Moreover, consistently enforcing those rules and monitoring their behaviour help to reduce the likelihood of underage drinking.

Control Your Outburst

Even when you hear something about your kid's underage drinking experiment or habit that upsets you, hold your horses. Take a few deep breaths before you speak as losing your temper and giving an immediate tongue-lashing will prove detrimental. We need to counter anger or our own feeling of guilt when faced with a grim situation, for neither is helpful. What is likely to work is a frank and patient conversation with children, where we express our feelings in a positive way without hastening to label them as 'bad'. Most importantly, we must prioritize their safety and let them know that no matter what, they should first come to us, in case of any deviation.

Education is Crucial

Educating adolescents about how alcohol affects their body and organs is important. In fact, it should be part of their academic curriculum. Let your teenager know that he or she can talk to you about anything, without judgement or lecturing. Also, talk frankly about family instances to them. If your family has had problems with alcohol, your child should know about them. Be open about your own experiences too.

Get to Know Your Teen's Friends

Every parent must make concerted efforts to be familiar with their children's friends. Getting to know their friends and parents better will help us understand our teenager's world.

Even as parents employ all their energies, intelligence and tact to keep the children from falling into the rut of underage drinking, there can be aberrations. But when the wrong keeps getting repeated despite all checks, it is advisable to seek swift professional help of a counsellor or a doctor.

18

Train Them to Handle Adversity

'Hidden in trouble lies the key to our magnificent opportunity.'

—ALBERT EINSTEIN

Social scientists across the world are trying to find out why this generation of youngsters, brilliant at understanding and decoding technology, is unable to resolve its problems with similar ease. Despite possessing the best amenities and the most elite gadgets, youngsters today continue to be bogged down by depression and despondency. This is primarily because we, as parents, have left no stone unturned to provide them the finest food, excellent education and every other luxury, but forgotten to teach them how to handle adversities.

Says famous author and organizational expert Stephen Covey: 'Just as we develop our physical muscles through overcoming opposition—such as lifting weights—we develop our character muscles by overcoming challenges and adversity.' In order to set our children up for success, we have to prepare them by giving the confidence to work through adversity.

Interestingly, it is this adversity quotient, or AQ, that discerning employers are now looking for in prospective candidates over and above their IQs (intelligence quotient) and EQs (emotional quotient). The ability for crisis management is increasingly being considered crucial whether in driving up sales or satisfying customers.

Adversity Quotient
Have you ever thought, what is that trait which goads one person

to shrug off repeated setbacks and try again, while the other gives up on the slightest hint of failure? It is resilience or the ability to bounce back from adversity. Even though parents wish their children were equipped with the wherewithal to handle adverse situations that life is bound to spring on them every once in a while, they seldom do anything about it.

Resilience is one attribute that parents must consciously foster in their kids right from early childhood. Or else any setback, unfortunate event or accident can break them and make them give up on life.

This resilience or the grit to take on adversity comes by developing the feeling 'I can handle this' or 'No matter what happens, I can find a solution'. This is what Rancho (Aamir Khan's character in the film *3 Idiots*) advised his friends to repeat to themselves—'All is well, all is well'—to tide over difficult situations.

Benefits of Resilience

We know the world can be a frightening place. With all the uncertainties in life pertaining to death, illness, war, crime, natural calamities and terrorism, one is often faced with situations which have the potential to break or scar our souls. Families, especially children, are under tremendous stress with the potential to damage both physical health and psychological well-being. While it is not easy to protect them from the ups and downs of life, it is certainly possible to raise tough children who can be equipped with the skills to handle the unexpected.

Resilient kids, who have the potential to face adverse situations and bounce back, are great planners and problem solvers, say experts. Children, who face and overcome all kinds of difficult situations, fare better in their lives as grown-ups. For example, Oprah Winfrey, the only African-American woman to be part of the Forbes billionaire list in 2017, has repeatedly admitted to having not just an impoverished but also a traumatic childhood. Research shows they have stronger marriages and better health than those who have hardly faced difficult situations. They are also less likely to face emotional problems.

Some of us can identify this with our parents or grandparents who had it tough in life. They studied with great hardships, barely managed two square meals a day and rarely had new clothes to wear. Now, all these people would have grown up to be not just successful, but also tough individuals equally adept at handling pain, loss and deprivation.

Unfortunately, most people who come up the hard way, usually try to make it as easy as possible for their children. As a result, they lose their grip on life when faced with the slightest discomfort or setback. That explains the alarming rise in cases of depression, suicides and homicides among the youth, particularly those of the well-endowed.

Significantly, unlike genetics, resilience can be moulded. Each of us as parents, teachers and caregivers of children can work to develop that inner resolve among them to not give up when confronted with hurdles and failures, misgivings and criticisms or rejection and heartbreak.

Teenage Crushes Can Crush Lives

Rejection and heartbreaks incidentally form a part and parcel of growing up years. A crush is something practically every individual experiences in his adolescence. It involves an awakening of special romantic feelings towards another person—adolescent or adult. Since it has more to do with fantasy than reality, it usually wears off in a short time. But, as long as it lasts, it consumes the teen's world, creating a complex web of emotions and anxiety. Hence, experts like Prakash and Ghosal warn parents not to take it lightly or make fun of it.

Some time back, when Ranchi was rocked by the brutal killing of a 12-year-old, it once again hit home the fact that teenage crushes can assume catastrophic proportions, if not handled judiciously by adults. The Class VII student of a reputed boarding school was bludgeoned by his love interest's teen brother who was averse to the relationship.[29] The subsequent bid by the girl's family to cover up the murder, in fact, had an uncanny resemblance to Ajay Devgn's *Drishyam*. In the film, however, the teen was a stalker, the spoilt son of a police commissioner, who was killed inadvertently by the girl when he came up with an indecent proposal.

The tragedy in Ranchi, incidentally, was not a one-off case as every other day we come across instances of teenage love gone wrong. The outcome often varies from nervous breakdown and depression to acid attack and suicide. Every incident only underlines how we repeatedly fail as the older generation to read the distress signals and act on time.

It's often easy to recognize tell-tale signs of a crush with your girl as she begins sporting a dreamy faraway look and loves scribbling the name of the person concerned behind notebooks.

---

[29]'12-year-old boy killed for crush on teacher's kid in Ranchi', *The Telegraph*, 11 February 2016, http://www.abplive.in/india-news/12-year-old-boy-killed-for-crush-on-teachers-kid-in-ranchi-288342

As long as it doesn't affect her grades and normal activities, it's better to let her be. Boys, in contrast, are more cagey about their feelings and end up with more intense actions and reactions. While most crushes end as abruptly as they begin, as parents and guardians, we need to help them deal with the situation in a positive manner.

> **Handling Crushes**
>
> - First and foremost, parents must make themselves available for their children and create the comfort level for a frank talk with them. If a teen shares the details of his/her crush, it is advisable not to be alarmed.
> - Since having a crush evokes mixed feelings, youngsters often don't know how to handle themselves, leave aside deal with the object of their affection. So, it's a good idea to discuss what they can do and avoid doing.
> - Sometimes when we acknowledge their obsessive behaviour as normal, it helps ease their discomfort and awkwardness. Talking about your own teenage crush also helps them feel normal. However, focus more on listening than talking.
> - While girls are more vocal, boys mostly keep it to themselves and so experience a rougher roller coaster of emotions. It is imperative to teach them when to back off and in any eventuality never to stalk their interest.
> - Since everyone believes their crush to be a serious relationship, it is advisable never to make fun of their feelings. Tell the teens to enjoy the euphoria as long as it lasts. A day would come when they would share these stories with their own children.[30]

---

[30]'Don't let crushes crush their lives', 20 February 2016. Source: The Times of India Group. © BCCL. All Rights Reserved

Ways to Build Buoyancy

Besides romantic liaisons gone awry, there can be several other adverse situations in the lives of children—from failure in exams and competitions to betrayal and loss of reputation. Despite our best efforts, we cannot prevent hard times for us or our children. But, we can change how we perceive challenges and adversities.

I particularly loved spiritual leader, Dada J.P. Vaswani's views on troubles. Problems are like pebbles, he says, they look magnified if you hold close to the eyes and become small when put at a distance. 'They are actually presents wrapped in a soiled paper.' Just ignore the wrapping and focus on the gift. Each of them helps us grow as they offer opportunities for development, says the elderly mystic.

So, we need to repeatedly tell our children that tests, trials and tribulations are bound to be there. No matter what we go through, we must believe they will turn out for our good. It's only then, says author Billi Lim in his interesting book *Dare to Fail*, that burdens become blessings and trials become triumphs.

Some Measures to Build Resilience

- Encourage your child to develop positive and effective coping strategies. Teach them to figure out solutions of everyday problems themselves.
- Empowering children to make decisions goes a long way in building their confidence.
- We can help the development of competence by helping children focus on individual strengths. Clearly express their best qualities such as integrity, perseverance and kindness.
- Teach your child to lose gracefully. Often parents themselves are unwilling to accept failures. So, kids too begin to react violently.

Train Them to Handle Adversity

- Teach kids to handle their emotions. While it is all right to feel angry, sad or hurt, what is more importantly needed is to figure out the next step.
- Developing close ties with family and community creates a solid sense of security which in turn leads to strong values and prevents alternative destructive paths to love and attention.
- Help your child understand that life's events are not purely random and that most things are an outcome of past choices and actions. They must know that the bigger picture, which they are unable to see for now, will unfold only gradually and they ought to be patient.
- Last but not least, we need to model positive coping strategies on a consistent basis as kids also learn from observing their parents' behaviour. We cannot afford to tell them to control their outbursts, while we keep flipping out at the slightest provocation.

As adults, we come to know that life is the sum total of good and bad times. Storms are bound to appear in terms of a missed opportunity, a heartbreak or loss of life. What we need to reinforce is the wisdom that every hardship is so designed to make us emerge as stronger and wiser.

After all, tough houses that last for centuries are built not by raw bricks, but by those that are baked over fire to make them sturdy.

19

Clip Complacency, Egg Them On to Dream

> *'All our dreams can come true,*
> *if we have the courage to pursue them.'*
>
> —WALT DISNEY

Rita Basu, the founder principal of Disharee, a famous Montessori school in South Kolkata once remarked, 'You know, children of economically less endowed parents are far more enthusiastic in life. They carry out instructions much better than those of the privileged ones.' Having worked as a successful educator for over four decades, she was not off the mark in her observation.

As the spouse and I pondered the lady's comment over our Sunday morning cuppa, we noted how children from modest backgrounds were increasingly doing better for themselves. The day's newspaper headlines only seemed to endorse our observation as it announced the rare feat of a vegetable seller's son, Mariyappan Thangavelu, who won the first gold for India at the 2016 Rio Paralympics. It was an inspiring and heart-warming story of a highly motivated youngster, who outshone poverty as well as his debility to grab success, all for his mother—a single parent.

Several such instances of children living in shanties, studying under street lamps, using borrowed books and making it big for themselves by cracking the IIT, medical or the haloed IAS entrance exams, are becoming rather common. Our milkman's son, for instance, is pursuing Law at a premier institute, while his nephew cracked the 'tough' MBBS entrance exams to get the college of his choice in Kolkata.

One of the primary reasons behind these incredible success stories is the determination to lead a better life. These children are fired by a strong urge to realize the dreams of their underprivileged parents, who sacrifice a major slice of their livelihood to sustain their studies. In contrast to these highly driven, focused and diligent youngsters, who are egged on by their aspirational stirrup, are the chilled out, complacent children of the privileged lot. Call it the perils of prosperity or whatever, but most kids of affluent or even upper middle classes today are overindulged, bored and shifty. Used to every kind of luxury in life, they often lack the drive to push themselves beyond their comfort levels.[31]

Moreover, as experts like Brahmachari point out, the moral and emotional hazards of growing up rich include increasing substance abuse and indulging in self-inflicting behaviour, both by adolescents as well as young adults. To add to the ills of having everything laid out on a platter are the high levels of distractions that our youngsters constantly need to tackle.

Counter Complacency

Thankfully, there are solutions at hand, but require perseverance and a tough willpower to counter initial failures. Even as they provide children with all amenities in life, parents need to emphasize on responsibility and accountability. Linking

---

[31]'Parenteen: Jog them out of complacency, focus on responsibility', 19 September 2016. Source: The Times of India Group. © BCCL. All Rights Reserved

behaviour and performances to natural consequences can be useful as it helps people (not just teens) take responsibility for their actions.

Moreover, we need to help children gain perspective on their own privileged state which they often seem to take for granted. This can be done practically by ensuring interactions with the less endowed people around them. Taking them on regular trips to the slums and orphanages helps to create that insight on the realities of life, besides evoking compassion in them. Psychologists claim it also induces warmer relationships among family members.

Nudge Them to Dream

Every child has a unique set of strengths. Now, it is the duty of the parents to identify and draw attention to them and most importantly help them realize their potential. Some children display their forte as childhood passions which, if identified and suitably channelized, can turn out to be their calling. A nephew, who spent his boyhood making sketches of every car in his neighbourhood with unique imaginary features, went on to study design in Italy. Today he's a sought-after product designer with a passion to improvise on the mundane.

Aamir Khan's magnum opus *Dangal*, besides being an entertaining real-life sports flick, offered some amazing lessons on parenting, that too through a simple villager from Haryana. For the uninitiated, the film charted the journey of two sisters—wrestling champions Geeta Phogat and Babita Kumari—who were egged on by their father to break the skewed notions about the girl child. While many condemned Mahavir Singh

Phogat for loading his daughters up with his own aspirations, he did not care two hoots about the criticisms. For, if not for his nudge, the Phogat girls, who are known to have made a mark in international wrestling, would have ended up as child brides like their friends.

Helping our children to first dream and then live out their dreams is critical to effective parenting. For children, parents are their primary motivators and leaders. Agrees Cedric M. Kenny, a winner's profile is truly wrapped around the support system provided by the parents. 'Motivation is the quintessence of all ingredients that makes winners,' he explains. Parents need to renew the motivation mantra day after day so that children stay focused and enjoy completing every task. Experts suggest asking oneself, 'Am I giving due attention and support to the competence that naturally exists in my teen?'

Mantra for Success

It is rightly observed that winners and achievers are not born, they are made. After identifying the spark in children, parents and guardians need to judiciously work on it to transform them into frontrunners.

Following certain techniques can prove effective to evolve the winner in your child:

a. Introduce them to the power of visualization

It involves getting the child to clearly imagine in the mind's eye where and how he would want to see himself in future. Goad him on to share the details of his dreams with you and visualize himself living out those dreams. This is what experts term as the power of visualization which acts as a stir-up for realization of goals. Children, who possess the vision and the drive to achieve their dreams, have higher resilience and are more likely to make wise choices in life. So, as parents of prospective achievers, we have to ignite that fire in their bellies to go all out to seek their dreams.

b. Keep up the appreciation

The second step involves showing appreciation for every small achievement of youngsters. At the same time, it is equally important to acknowledge and appreciate every small effort in that direction. Sometimes, they may not achieve success, but praising their persistence even if they need to do much more will keep them on the job. Never demoralize kids; remember, they are yet to realize their potential. They have to set high standards for themselves and learn to compete with themselves to bring out their best.

c. Create opportunities to support their endeavour

We must encourage children to explore different activities and opportunities in order to give them a broad spectrum of experiences. Let them discover their own interests. A relative's son is a sports enthusiast, who began training for basketball when he was only six years old. As an adolescent, he evinced interest in cricket and his parents enrolled him for cricket lessons after school. Mornings before school were marked for marathon running along with his father. When I asked the parents about the reason behind pursuing multiple activities, they explained they had recognized a sporty streak in him. They were exposing him to different kinds of sports so he could pick and pursue the one he would eventually realize he was best at. Besides learning what it takes to master every sport, the kid has had an amazing grounding in resilience.

d. Help in setting goals and charting out their roadmap

In order to transform children into effective achievers, encourage them to set up goals. Help them chart out a roadmap so they know exactly the way to go and adopt necessary changes along the journey. Teaching them the importance of time management is equally important. Do not forget to inculcate a sense of routine by adhering to a definite timetable.

e. Tap the power of the subconscious

Both scientists as well as spiritual masters emphasize the immense power of our thoughts and point out that the treasure house is within us. Think good and good will follow; negative thoughts will lead to negative actions. Change your thoughts to change your destiny, says Joseph Murphy in *The Power of Your Subconscious Mind*. When we keep our conscious mind busy with expectations of the best, our subconscious will faithfully reproduce our habitual thinking, he says.

Similarly, Sister Shivani of the Brahma Kumaris emphasizes watching our thoughts as they affect every cell of the body. 'Every thought I create is energy that I'm transmitting,' she says and insists on maintaining a complete harmony between words and thoughts. For instance, even if we keep saying, 'Go ahead, you can do it', but our minds are filled with doubts like 'I don't think he can do it because...' the child will never be able to do it. So, it is crucial to first train ourselves and then our children to always think positive and reap the harvests of positivity.

f. Practise self-control techniques

Another essential step to bring out winners in your teens is to build self-control so that kids are able to focus on their goals. Practising regular focusing sessions and adopting concentration-building activities like watching the breath, yoga and meditation can aid in bringing a sense of purpose amid distractions.

g. Convince them to focus on themselves

When we train children to focus on themselves, they put all their energies in pushing themselves ahead, instead of getting distracted by what others are doing and saying. During a race, this is the mantra given by coaches to the athletes—to just look ahead at the finishing line.

h. Practise mindful living

In today's world of high-speed action, most of us seem to function on autopilot. According to Dada J.P. Vaswani, 80 per cent of the mind is engaged in thinking about the past, 15 per cent on the future and only 5 per cent is in the present. Multitasking is indeed a bane of the modern world. Dada Vaswani narrates an incident about a saint who was asked to reveal the secret of greatness. The saint replied: 'When I eat, I eat; when I work, I work and when I sleep, I sleep.' In today's world we actually eat without tasting the food, talk without attention and work with hundreds of thoughts rummaging through our minds. Mindful living entails living in the present and desisting from multitasking.

When the mind is not plagued by past misgivings and fears of the future, but is focused on present endeavours, success comes naturally.

20
Instil Spiritual Grounding

*'Those who bring sunshine to the lives of others
cannot keep it from themselves.'*

—JAMES M. BARRIE

When we sent Anukriti to a spiritual youth camp, there was major furore in our extended family. 'Her behaviour is perfectly normal, like any other teenager, what is the need to punish her with this spiritual treatment? Moreover, this is certainly no age to go to an ashram,' went the harried admonitions. We tried in vain to assuage their apprehensions as we had done our homework on the organization and were suitably convinced before enrolling. Nevertheless, we reached the camp venue with some trepidation as going against every senior member in the family was not too palatable. The only face-saving factor was our girl's cool composure who viewed it as just another exercise at self-improvement.

To cut a long story short, we stood vindicated. When I went to collect her on the final day, I could hear gleeful sounds of music and drums. 'No disco in the world could match up with the ecstatic fun we had singing and dancing to bhajans,' she gushed in breathless excitement. Their days were filled with interesting sessions on handling stress, studies, exams, fitness, service (*seva*) and meditation, among other things. I encountered scores of parents who were regulars at the camp every year. They conceded that the spiritual foundation had worked wonders for their children in terms of building confidence, concentration, sense of discipline and

Instil Spiritual Grounding

time management, apart from reducing stress and anger issues.

A few days on, I asked Anukriti about her prime takeaway from that camp. 'I feel more at ease with myself and happy for no reason, in particular,' she replied nonchalantly. Although the feeling lasted for quite some time, clearly it was not a one-time fix.

Good for the Young Too

Spirituality is usually associated with several myths—that it's for the elderly who have nothing left to do or for the distressed souls who seek divine redemption. It actually involves a sense of connection with something bigger than us—with God, nature or even art. In a world, which is increasingly turning more and more egocentric, it's this higher connect which can keep us grounded and help accept the vicissitudes of life with humility. Spirituality brings about the ability to accept, adjust and accommodate, thereby empowering us in the process. As one begins to look at life and situations objectively, solutions to problems begin to emerge from within.

Two crucial aspects of a spiritual foundation include yoga and meditation. While yoga entails exercise of the mind and body, meditation involves travelling inwards by silencing the cacophony of thoughts that constantly besiege the mind. Both have proved immensely valuable for the mental and physical well-being of the youth and the elderly alike. Yet enrolling for yoga or a spiritual camp is not as preferable among youngsters who would rather spend their time and fortune on, for instance, image-enhancing endeavours.

A Shot of Humility is Must

Another vital component of spirituality, which is also recognized as its byproduct, is humility—a quality of being courteously respectful of others. In this age, where pride and arrogance are bountiful and come in rather early, humbleness is certainly a rarity. It is discomforting to notice how even small children today give superfluous importance to the cars their parents drive, the quality of toys they possess or brands they sport on their bodies. If not nipped in the bud, this early display of smugness eventually develops into self-importance and arrogance as teens grow into adults. No wonder, India is known for its 'don't-you-know-who-I-am' syndrome. That's probably the root cause of brawls involving celebrities or politicians, whether at cricket stadiums, hotels or pubs.

Today, as we encounter arrogance in practically every sphere—from road rage and blatant traffic violations to inconsiderate behaviour for others in public places—there is an urgent need to kindle humbleness and restraint among our children. But one can teach humility only by setting an example.

Two important tools that bring about humility are gratitude and apology. Gratefulness and the ability to admit one's mistakes and say sorry are often hard to come by, especially as one rises in rank and affluence. I think this is primarily because we do not practise these traits naturally at home, with spouses, children, or the people who serve us daily. A reality check at how many times you say 'thank you' or 'sorry' to the spouse or children can reveal the truth in this statement. Mind you, this does not mean being formal with family members, it's merely shaking off your ingrained mindset of superiority. When we practise saying

Instil Spiritual Grounding

'please', 'thank you' and 'sorry' to each other at home, it nurtures humility, besides creating a warm and loving atmosphere. Do try this at home!

When humility combines with discipline, great accomplishments come by in abundance.

Teach Them to Pray to and Connect with God

This point is applicable to only those who believe in God. It is all right if you don't.

Some young people, in fact, think it is cool to be an atheist and frown upon those who believe in God. On the other hand, some follow a religion without realizing what they actually believe. Pastor and inspirational speaker Samir Deokuliar says: 'The fact is that everyone believes. An atheist too believes—he believes there is No God. So whichever way you go, you do believe. The choice you need to make is what do you believe and do you really believe what you think you believe?'

Most of us accept God as the source of all power and believe in Him. And children often grow up watching their parents pray, celebrate religious festivals and perform certain rituals. While some follow suit, some question it as dogma. As belonging to the older and wiser generation, I feel parents must talk about the presence or the importance of that Supreme Being in our lives. God is relevant and Spirituality is relevant in this generation. As we openly discuss the reasons behind the faith we follow we must remember to emphasize upon the need to respect all other faiths too. At the same time we also need to explain that rituals are meant as reminders to infuse core values like purity of thoughts, honesty, unity and compassion in our daily lives.

It is advisable to encourage children to read, understand, experience and then develop their faith in God. Guide them to remove various labels attached with God and focus on creating a direct personal relationship with Him. Only then will they be able to close their eyes in a sincere prayer and reach out to Him in moments of pain and stress, particularly in the absence of parents.

A friend narrated how a small photo frame of her Guruji and the habit of praying that she instilled in her son as a boy saved his life while studying engineering far away from home. The boy confessed to her how one day, overcome by depression, he was on the verge of committing suicide. As he stood in front of the photo before taking the final plunge, he claimed to have suddenly been shaken out of his stupor of despair and the enormity of his decision dawned upon him.

Train Them to be Givers

In this busy world, where time is expensive, doing our bit for philanthropy usually entails mailing donations or signing cheques for organizations which promptly offer tax benefits in return. Unfortunately, besides losing out on an enriching experience of an actual interaction with the less endowed, it fails to impact our children. They continue to lead their lives of ever-mounting needs, seeking instant gratification. But, when we give as a family—our time, attention and money—it registers with them the need to give.

Actions are a powerful teacher, say Azim Jamal and Harvey McKinnon in their book, *The Power of Giving*. Children, who are taught to be kind, grow up to be caring adults. I have always felt that elderly parents, who complain their children have forsaken them, have a lot to blame themselves for their fate. If only they had instilled virtues of compassion and generosity in them as children, things would have, perhaps, been different. Taking out time to visit an old age home or orphanage and meet street children or the destitute sleeping on pavements often make us realize that giving is far more joyful than getting. I know of this youngster (in his twenties) who, along with a handful of his friends from IIT, Delhi, spends the New Year's Eve not at pubs or clubs but distributing blankets to people sleeping on the pavements in Old Delhi. Encouraging generosity and thoughtfulness in kids can entail simple deeds like getting them to donate a portion of their pocket money, making 'thank you' cards for teachers and friends or teaching children from underprivileged families. The act may not require any money, but just a few moments of selflessness. When we encourage children to nurture this habit of giving little things in life—their time or pocket money—for any social cause, we subtly help them learn the important trait of empathy.

It also helps to let the youngsters know that what goes around—a good deed—comes around.

Decode the Significance of Festivals

Over the years, festivals have come to be associated only with mindless shopping and acquiring every material good on earth that money can buy. No wonder, we find corporate majors and advertising consultants wooing customers with the best of deals. Lost in this maze of attractive offers, we often miss out on the true meaning and symbolism behind the festivals.

I think it makes good sense to apprise our youngsters and bear in our minds too, the spiritual significance of festivals, be it Holi, Deepavali, Christmas or Eid. For instance, we all know Navratra and Dussehra signify the victory of good over evil, the killing of the demon Mahishasura by Goddess Durga. These epic legends actually symbolize the profound analogy that both Goddess Shakti and demon Mahishasura (the good and the evil) reside within us. The festival calls for efforts to awaken this Shakti within to purge the inner demons of anger, greed, lust, pride and ego.

As a child, I often used to wonder why we worshipped Goddess Lakshmi on Diwali as we were told it was Lord Rama who returned after fourteen years of exile on this day to Ayodhya upon killing demon king Ravana. Our teachers explained that the festival got its name Deepavali from the rows of earthen lamps that the people of Ayodhya lit to welcome their beloved king. It wasn't until much later that I came to know Diwali is also celebrated to mark the incarnation of Goddess Lakshmi, the divine strength of Lord Vishnu whom she married on this darkest night of the year (*Amavasya*). The earthen lamps signify our quest to end the darkness of ignorance and everything negative or evil.

Besides, acquainting children with the insightful reasons behind festivals, one can also encourage them to find out more about the rituals that are practised. Most have deep-seated scientific or logical explanations. For instance, offering puffed rice to Goddess Lakshmi signifies prosperity as the Kharif crop is ready for harvest around Diwali. Likewise, the bonfire on the eve of Holi denotes burning away negativity, anger and ego, followed by the celebration of belief in God by playing with colours. Similarly, the ritual of having a hearty traditional meal with family and friends in all religious festivals underlines the significance of laughter and togetherness in life.

21

Strive to Provide a Loving Home

'If you would be loved, love and be lovable.'

—BENJAMIN FRANKLIN

One weekend, we were pleasantly surprised to find an old acquaintance from another city at our door. We had been married around the same time, but had lost touch after moving cities. Following tea and pleasantries, he explained he was in town to meet his 16-year-old daughter who lived with her mother. The couple had separated some time back and each had settled down with another life partner. When we inquired about his child, he fished out his cell phone to show his daughter's picture. It was a charming girl dressed in trendy wear but with a set of distinctly painful eyes. As a parent, I seemed to be able to perceive the anguish of a child who witnessed an acerbic separation of the two most important pillars of her life. The friend confessed there was still substantial tension between the two of them. Quite evidently, it was deeply affecting the child.

As they bring up their children, the role of parents tends to assume more importance for they act as mirrors through which children not only see themselves, but to a great extent even the world outside. The manner in which parents behave with each other remains in the child's psyche and tends to determine his/her perception of the world. That is to say, the relationship between parents has a profound impact on the mental and physical health of kids. When husbands and wives function as a team, there is less possibility of troubled or unhappy children.[32]

Cops concede when they trace the history of delinquents, more often than not, they appear to have had troubled childhoods with estranged, violent or warring parents behind them. However, when separating couples manage to keep the well-being of children above their personal differences or part on cordial terms, the children are less likely to experience distress.

Work as a Team

From the time a child is born, it is very important for family members to have a common agreement on corrections. Everyone at home should agree on what is acceptable behaviour and what is not. If parents constantly fight and contradict each other, they fill the child's brain with confusion, negativity and insecurity.

In most families, particularly in India, inconsistent parenting is a major problem as both parents often override each other's decisions. Add to that the crucial role of overindulgent grandparents and the children end up growing in an environment of utter confusion related to family values and discipline. Soon, they learn to use one against the other for their trivial advantages.

Homemaker Rini* confesses to losing her cool with her husband Nikhil* and his parents who repeatedly override the rule of 'no television on weekdays' for her two boys. She claims to often find herself isolated when it comes to disciplining her children who she fears are becoming increasingly wild mannered

---

[32]'Parenteen: Work as team with spouse', 12 February 2017, Source: The Times of India Group. © BCCL. All Rights Reserved

and ill-tempered.

Repeated arguments and squabbles between parents or grandparents have an immense negative impact on the behaviour of children, concede psychologists. Moreover, bad behaviour between parents often gets ingrained in the children's psyche. Marriage counsellors claim that a fair number of couples, who come for divorce, reminisce the violent relationship between their parents and divulge an unexpressed rage inside them. It is important for both father and mother to constantly operate as a team. Their roles are unique and different and cannot overlap. Sharing the responsibilities of parenting between husband and wife leads to bringing up positive, healthy and self-reliant children. Both spouses need to support and complement each other and fill in where the other lags. For instance, while the mother keeps a tab on the diet and discipline, the father monitors academics and sports or vice versa.

A family that functions on the firm foundations of love, understanding and belief in each other, creates effective support systems for one another to succeed. Children from such families display positive traits like sacrifice, tolerance and acceptance which come more than handy when they step into the world as adults.

Spend Quality Time With Your Children

It is equally important to spend fair amount of quality time with our children. When we give time to our children, we not only strengthen our bond with them, but make them feel important which, in turn, enhances their self esteem.

Check out the joy and comfort on the faces of not just

children, but even teenagers and young adults when parents make time to attend important events involving the former. I still savour the heady feeling I experienced watching my parents from the stage when I won best actor in a school play. The picture of my dad clapping the hardest long after the audience had stopped or my mom wiping her tears of happiness remains imprinted as one of the most stirring memories of my childhood.

'I advise parents not to bother so much about giving expensive gifts to children,' says Nandini Choudhury Brahmachari. 'Instead, focus on doing creative activities, playing games and sharing camaraderie,' advises the counsellor. Children are bound to get hurt, angry or scared as they interact with the outside world. But, they should have the comfort of coming home to their own world where they get due attention and appreciation.

Both parents must make an effort to attend school functions, be it a PTM, sports day, a science fair or an investiture ceremony for their induction into the students' council. Teachers concede that faces of their students shine twice as brightly when they glean the silhouettes of both parents even in the darkness of the school auditorium.

Handle Discord Prudently

To be honest, differences of opinion between two people, who live under the same roof, are bound to exist. While most experts and psychologists advise parents never to be at loggerheads in front of their children, I often feel it's a difficult proposition. For, even when parents thrash out the matter away from the kids' eyes, children are bound to get a feel of the 'cold war' which might ensue. So, what is more important is how we handle our tiffs and disagreements in front of the children.

'We cannot afford to keep children in a bubble,' agrees Nandini Choudhury Brahmachari. 'I feel one should not shy away from exposing the teenagers to discords within the household. They should know even warm and loving adults can have differences of opinion.' But, parents should remember to maintain decorum and cordiality even in their fights. There can be no name calling, use of abusive language or violence in any form.

Children need to observe how you resolve differences. When you have a discussion, follow author Stephen Covey's advice: 'Seek first to understand than be understood'. Most of the time, we are unwilling to be wrong or proved wrong, making it a matter about prestige. Be clear about your opinions, but accept that other people may have different and equally valid ones too. This is an important lesson that children learn by watching the relationship between their parents. As they witness how parents give in (once the father, another time the mother), make up and woo each other to change the atmosphere of animosity into warmth, they learn a significant lesson in life: every relationship, which succeeds, requires some degree of compromise on both sides.

Sit Down for Meals Together

A family meal is one of those things that may not seem like such a big deal, but it can make a huge difference for our children in terms of building their self-esteem, and creating a sense of security and happiness.

Although experts across the world recommend having at

least one meal together, with working parents, busy children and the differential tastes and timings of the two, it has become a difficult proposition today. Most households have children preferring to eat meals in their own rooms. The parents don't mind that for they too would rather have their meals while watching their favourite soap on the television or with friends, clients and colleagues.

Once when Anukriti had her friend over to spend the day, I found the youngster intently watching all the banter happening at the dining table. Our teen later revealed her friend found it interesting to see all of us sitting down together for a meal. She'd never realized it could be so much fun eating with the family.

The significance of sitting down together for meals was laid in my childhood, but it rubbed in deeper when pointed out by our guest. Actually, when we sit down together at a designated place, we give each other due time and attention. The conversations we have, or the sharing of experiences that take place, help us connect with each other and create that crucial family bonding. As children uninhibitedly narrate the day's events, parents actually get a peek into their minds.

Speaking for myself, I get to monitor food habits of my children ensuring they have their *dal* and greens too. Moreover, as the spouse and I narrate our childhood tales, address unfounded fears and misconceptions, we subtly manage to communicate to the children our core values in life.[33] In fact, studies increasingly point out to multiple benefits of family

---

[33]'Parenteen: Do you sit for a meal together?', 13 November 2016. Source: The Times of India Group. © BCCL. All Rights Reserved

meals for both children as well as parents. While it is credited for boosting the confidence of children, lowering their eating disorders and improving achievement scores, for the parents, it is known to typically reduce the tension levels. But an important prerequisite is to put aside all technological distractions like television, laptops and smartphones. Moreover, parents need to be warm and engaging instead of controlling and restrictive.

If having a meal together every day appears difficult, one can earmark specific days in the week. These family lunches or dinners may not be gourmet meals, but should have a notion of fun and relaxation about them. It's a good idea to follow them up with activities like a game of scrabble or word power, karaoke or a movie.

It certainly helps to keep in mind that family meals are probably the best psychological vitamins parents can give their children.

22

Adapt Your Parenting Style

'All you need is love.'

—JOHN LENNON

Parenting is indeed a full-time job which requires us to be physically, mentally and monetarily involved 24x7. The result of all the hard work may not be evident soon. But, unlike all other jobs, there is no greater reward than watching our children step into the world full of courage, confidence and compassion.

While most parents work for a common goal, they differ on their parenting styles, particularly in the teenage years. Some may be autocratic (restrictive with kids), others authoritarian (give independence, but within limits). Some are permissive (allow kids to do what they feel like) while others may be disinterested (ignoring kids). Psychologists agree good parenting methods not just in childhood, but through teenage and early adulthood, help children develop into well-rounded personalities.

Most parents bring up their children the way they were brought up, relying on pleasant and unpleasant childhood memories. It is common to hear: 'In our times, we never dared to question our elders' or 'We were so sacred of our father. Every time he walked in, we would quickly disappear'. But, it is unreasonable and even regressive to continue with antiquated notions about parenting. As times change, practically everything—from technology to our thinking—needs to be updated and modernized. So, parents too need to adapt their methods of bringing up children according to changing times, instead of merely following what their parents and grandparents did. After all, parenting is all about nurturing.

Change Stereotypical Beliefs

Today, most parents are stretching their means to provide the best of everything to their children—from education and food to clothing and gadgets. But, they are also bogging the kids down with their archaic belief systems. For instance, when we keep reminding our children, 'There's tough competition out there', we are only teaching them to constantly compare themselves with others, instead of focusing on themselves. Similarly, profound observations like 'Life is a struggle, one must fight it out' or 'Life is never fair' immediately strike fear and insecurity in the minds of children.

Instead of parroting these oft-repeated negative notions, parents should exhort children to work hard, focus on their capacities and abstain from creating ill will for their peers and colleagues. Moreover, they should ensure that children respect them and not fear them. For, fear only induces timidity and anxiety which are not good for a healthy parent-child relationship.

In his *Change Your Thoughts, Change Your Life*, Wayne Dyer says that when confronted with any stressful situation, you should keep in mind that being stiff won't get you far, whereas being flexible will carry you through. So, parents need to change the way they think about strength and power. When they allow their viewpoints to be challenged and bend when necessary, they should know they are actually choosing strength.

Keep the Love Flowing—Hugs, Cuddles et al.

Love is a universal desire and no one can have enough of it. Children have to learn how to hold on to love, sustain it and become loving people themselves. When we demonstrate our love with hugs, it only reinforces the warmth.

Several psychologists emphasize that it is important to touch, hug or hold our children at least twelve times a day, especially when they wake up, return from school or look worried. A simple hug expresses love without using words and makes sure they feel cared and connected every day. Doctors, psychiatrists and counsellors across the world unanimously recommend parents to hug kids as often as they can. Studies have proved that hugging is healthy for the body, mind and soul. It boosts self-esteem and brings about a sense of security in a way no language can. An atmosphere where hugs are common makes parents approachable and empathetic.

Try and make yours a 'hugging family'—one which thrives on generous doses of hugs. Besides the regular wake up and good night hugs, there are welcome hugs, victory hugs (at even minor achievements at school or workplace), best-of-luck hugs and even sad and scared hugs. But, the high points are the family or group hugs on occasions of extreme happiness or sadness. Believe me, it has the power to multiply mirth or dispel despondency at an amazing speed! One can gauge the authenticity of the statement only when one actually tries it out. I know, holding teen sons or daughters in an embrace can be a difficult proposition as some of them tend to shun physical demonstrations of love, especially by parents. What we can do is find little excuses to at least hold their hands.

They will soon know parental touch is natural, comforting and irreplaceable.[34]

Nip Gender Bias in the Bud

'Stop crying like a girl, it's unbecoming of a boy', a friend once chided her 4-year-old son who was cranky after a fall in the park. I winced at the offhand comment by the friend, a management consultant. We often nurture these erroneous notions that boys have to be physically tough, while girls are essentially delicate and prone to crying. Small wonder that children of so-called modern parents grow up with such preconceived notions about gender.

Dr Latika Prakash says: 'Colour coding of pink for girls and blue for boys is just the tip of the iceberg of gender biases that we have been nurturing unconsciously for years.' How often we find ourselves picking up cars and guns as gifts for boys, while it's mostly dolls and dressing-up kits for girls. Our gender biases run so deep and start so early that it's hard to look beyond them even in our homes. A random survey among teens to gauge their preferences on the professional roles for men and women revealed they preferred men as politicians and women as caregivers or art directors. Beside sounding disconcerting, it only reveals the deep-seated biases that we unknowingly hand down to our subsequent generations.

Parents need to consciously start gender training early on with their kids. It is important to get them over gender-specific roles. While most Indian households have clear, traditionally

---

[34]'Parenteen: Empower with a hug', 5 December 2016. Source: The Times of India Group. © BCCL. All Rights Reserved

demarcated roles for the husband and wife (like wives clean and husbands run errands), it is wise to overlap the roles so that children do not grow up believing 'girls can't do this' or 'boys shouldn't do that'. Emphasize to your children that it's sensible to be able to cook, clean and run errands irrespective of their gender. Take a relook at how chores are assigned between your son and daughter and rotate them often. It is equally important to speak up, especially in front of our children, when we see someone making a gender-specific statement.

Act as a Role Model
In the course of parenting, we are often faced with challenging situations wherein kids find themselves in the dock as a result of their immaturity, impulsiveness or wrong decisions. It is how we conduct ourselves at this critical juncture that I think not only helps our children face the current crisis, but also helps equip them with a coping skill. **It's surprising how the influence of parents runs far deeper than we may think**. The temperament of parents invariably tends to determine the behaviour of children. If the parent is calm and stable, he/she induces confidence and security in the child. Conversely, if the parent is aggressive and overpowering, the child becomes unsure and fearful.

As parents and teachers exhort children to live by morals, they often forget to follow them in their own lives. Sister Shivani of the Brahma Kumaris narrates how once on her visit to a school, teenagers shared their grouses: 'Our parents scold us for fighting with siblings, but what about when they fight so aggressively among themselves?' said one while another asked, 'Why can't teachers also be fair and unbiased when they insist on our honesty and integrity?' Being a role model for truth telling might be one of the greatest gifts to our children. We cannot afford to constantly lie without batting an eyelid in front of them (say, calling ill at work to watch a cricket match) even as we lecture them on being truthful.

Nurture a Strong Seed

It is the moral responsibility of every parent to bring up emotionally strong children. Unfortunately today, while kids are intellectually and physically strong and socially well-equipped, they remain emotionally feeble. With a weak soul power, they are unable to bear even minor jolts in life with fortitude. Say, if they do not perform well or face a setback in a relationship, they tend to snap and give up on life very easily. So, instead of focusing merely on children's academic and co-curricular growth, parents must necessarily pay attention to nurturing a strong soul. After all, only if the seed is strong will it be able to look after itself when it grows into a tree.

Azim Jamal and Harvey McKinnon call it giving children the necessary heart fibre. Just as you need fibre in your body to maintain your health, you need fibre in your heart to maintain strength in a world where you are buffeted each day by problems. The core components of the heart fibre include compassion, self-control, respect and empathy. Children develop this fibre from their environment, peers, community, but most importantly from parents. Small wonder that successful parenting ranks among the toughest yet the most fulfilling jobs in the world as we have the onus of building not just great citizens, but great nations and civilizations too.

Epilogue

As a parent myself, I too often agonize about whether we are giving the right impetus and direction towards bringing up our two children. On certain days, one feels there's so much more one can do and gets restless at the inadequacies. Then God has His ways of sending reassurances.

One night, just when I was about to doze off, Smallie sneaked in and curled up in bed behind me. I was too sleepy, but relished the unexpected windfall of affection from our teen. 'Just wanted to tell you guys are doing a great job! And I promise you'll never regret your efforts,' she whispered in my ears. Her comforting words clearly dissolved the day's exhaustion as I smiled into a deep slumber.

Good parenting, as I have come to understand, does not necessarily involve following a rule book. It certainly helps to keep in mind that one size doesn't fit all. Just like no two individuals are alike, every child, every teen and every situation calls for differential approaches. The trick is to follow your gut, remain communicative and be ready to evolve with times.

Acknowledgements

I owe my parenting values to my mom, Renuka Prasad, who strived to imbue all four of her children with the power of love, empathy and music. Most significantly, she never raised her hand on any of us, despite provocations and the strains of parenting.

I am grateful to my dad, Nagendra Prasad, for being my Rock of Gibraltar—in supporting, encouraging and exhorting me to chase my dreams even when they clashed with his traditional ones.

I am lucky to have Anurag as my spouse who is the wind beneath my wings as well as the ground below my feet.

My two children Anukriti (Smallie) and Atharv have helped me evolve as a mother and human being. They fill my world with incredible mirth and meaning.

I would not have been doing what I am but for my brother Nishith, sisters Namrata and Sheelta and their spouses Vaishali, Rakesh and Vinay.

I owe it to my nieces and nephews too who have always tolerated me as an extra parent in their lives.

An extraordinary circle of friends who have cheered, challenged and cajoled me into lifting my spirits as well as my faculties is what I consider another blessing in my life. I am particularly indebted to Anupama, Shimoni and ex-colleague Raj Kumar for urging me to write this book, besides a troop of pals who filled me with their valuable inputs.

Acknowledgements

I am obliged to Manish Sharma for finding time to make illustrations for this handbook.

And last but not least, I will forever be grateful to Shambhu Sahu, Rinita Banerjee and Rupa Publications for selecting my brief, believing in me and giving me an opportunity to present my take on teenage parenting.

Thank you all for coming into my life and being a part of this endeavour!

Suggested Readings

Jamal, Azim, and Harvey McKinnon. *The Power of Giving*. Jaico Publishing House, 2008.

Murphy, Joseph. *The Power of Your Subconscious Mind*. Embassy Book Distributors, 2010.

Bharadia, Raksha. *Roots and Wings: A Handbook for Parents*. Rupa & Co., 2008.

Dyer, Wayne W. *Change Your Thoughts, Change Your Life: Living the Wisdom of the Tao*. Hay House, 2013.

Kenny, Cedric M. *Love Without Spoiling, Discipline Without Nagging: Toddlers to Teens*. Wisdom Tree, 2004.

Koran, Al. *Bring Out the Magic in Your Mind: The Worldwide Bestseller that can Launch You on the Road to Success*. Thorsons, 1998.

Lim, Billi P.S. *Dare to Fail: The Other Side of the Success Story*. Qford, 2013.

Mitra, Arpita. 'An Education for India: In the Footsteps of Sister Nivedita.' *Prabuddha Bharata*, vol. 122, no. 1, 2017, pp. 235–53.